THE ULTIMATE
OHIO STATE BUCKEYES
TRIVIA BOOK

A Collection of Amazing Trivia Quizzes and
Fun Facts for Die-Hard Buckeyes Fans!

Ray Walker

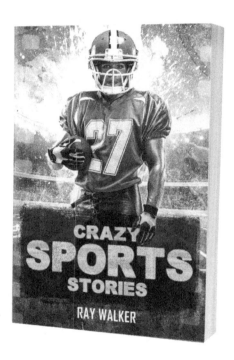

CONTENTS

INTRODUCTION

The Ohio State University played its first football game in the nineteenth century, unaware of the success that would follow the Buckeyes during the next two centuries. The Buckeyes have become the best program in the Big Ten over the last 120-plus years, dominating the conference for large stretches of its existence. Ohio State won that first game against Ohio Wesleyan, the first in 931 victories in the program's illustrious history. The critics can say what they want about the Buckeyes, but no matter who has been coaching them—especially over the last two decades—Ohio State has always been at the forefront of the national conversation when it comes to college football and is always a serious threat to win a national title.

This book attempts to cover the entire history of the Ohio State program from the first game day to the loss to Alabama in the 2020 National Championship Game. All of the highs, the occasional lows, and everything in between are all fair game to be included in this book, so be prepared to have your knowledge put to the test. We are going to quiz you on all of your favorite players and coaches over the next 12 chapters of fun facts and interesting nuggets, with the goal that you will finish this book knowing much more about your beloved

Buckeyes than when you picked it up. If we're successful, this is not going to be easy for you, but you will expand your knowledge base about the Buckeyes football program.

This book is designed to be a little difficult and keep you engaged and thinking as you ponder the history of this superb program. Each chapter in this book focuses on a specific topic, from the history of the program to specific positions and even the record book. In each chapter, there will be 20 multiple-choice or true-false questions, the answers to those questions (on a separate page), and 10 interesting tidbits about that chapter's topic that will hopefully shed some light on the behind-the-scenes information. So please do not be alarmed if some of these questions stump you; the whole point of the book is to help you learn more about your favorite team, so don't expect to ace every chapter.

We want you to learn something new after devouring this book so that you can use your newfound knowledge to show off to your fellow fans throughout the Midwest. All of the information is current as of the end of the 2020 season, so be warned that you might know more about the future by the time you pick up this book. All you need to do now is sit back, relax, and enjoy the hours of fun this book provides for the biggest Ohio State Buckeyes fans in the world.

CHAPTER 1:

ORIGINS & HISTORY

QUIZ TIME!

1. When did Ohio State face off with Ohio Wesleyan in the first game in program history?

   a. 1889

   b. 1890

   c. 1891

   d. 1892

2. Ohio State's first football game was played in May.

   a. True

   b. False

3. Though the Buckeyes didn't join the Big Ten until the 1913 season, who was the first Big Ten team Ohio State faced?

   a. Purdue

   b. Northwestern

   c. Michigan State

   d. Michigan

4. Who did Ohio State beat for its first official win in the Big Ten?

    a. Wisconsin
    b. Indiana
    c. Northwestern
    d. Illinois

5. Ohio State had to wait until 1895 to play a game outside the state of Ohio when they traveled to play which current FBS school?

    a. Pittsburgh
    b. Bowling Green
    c. Kentucky
    d. Ball State

6. In 1914, which Ohio State player was the first to be named an All-American?

    a. Lloyd Black
    b. Boyd Cherry
    c. Chic Harley
    d. Carl Rothgeb

7. In which season did Ohio State claim its first Big Ten championship?

    a. 1919
    b. 1918
    c. 1917
    d. 1916

8. Before playing at Ohio Stadium, the Buckeyes played next door at Ohio Field.

a. True

b. False

9. Ohio State made its debut in the Associated Press poll in 1936 when it entered the contest against Michigan at what ranking?

    a. 16

    b. 17

    c. 18

    d. 19

10. In which year did Ohio State first reach number one in the country?

    a. 1936

    b. 1938

    c. 1940

    d. 1942

11. Which team did Ohio State beat in 1952 for its first win over the number one team in the country?

    a. Cornell

    b. Wisconsin

    c. Michigan

    d. Army

12. Which team has Ohio State NOT played in the Big Ten championship game?

    a. Northwestern

    b. Nebraska

    c. Wisconsin

    d. Michigan State

13. Ohio State has a losing record in bowl games.

    a. True

    b. False

14. Against which school does Ohio State have the most wins without a loss?

    a. Washington State

    b. Ohio

    c. Oregon

    d. Florida State

15. Who did Ohio State play in 1985 in the first night game at Ohio Stadium?

    a. Michigan

    b. Pittsburgh

    c. Wisconsin

    d. Southern California

16. Before the pandemic canceling the 2020 matchup, when was the last time Ohio State did NOT end the regular season against Michigan?

    a. 1930

    b. 1934

    c. 1937

    d. 1942

17. Michigan is the only team to beat Ohio State more than 20 times.

    a. True

    b. False

18. What charm do Ohio State players receive for a win over Michigan?

   a. Gold "W"
   b. Silver jersey
   c. Gold buckeye
   d. Gold pants

19. Which of these non-sousaphone players did NOT have the honor of dotting the "i" during Script Ohio?

   a. Jack Nicklaus
   b. Archie Griffin
   c. John Glenn
   d. Woody Hayes

20. What is NOT a definition for a buckeye?

   a. Poisonous nut
   b. Burn the Priest song
   c. Candy
   d. Naval aircraft

QUIZ ANSWERS

1. B – 1890

2. A – True

3. D – Michigan

4. C – Northwestern

5. C – Kentucky

6. B – Boyd Cherry

7. D – 1916

8. A – True

9. C – 18

10. D – 1942

11. B – Wisconsin

12. B – Nebraska

13. A – True

14. C – Oregon

15. B – Pittsburgh

16. D – 1942

17. B – False

18. D – Gold pants

19. B – Archie Griffin

20. Trick question, it's all four!

DID YOU KNOW?

1. Before hiring John Wilce to coach the team, Ohio State struggled to keep a coach for more than one season. The Buckeyes went through five coaches in five years from 1909 through 1913 because a coach would have success and then resign. Ohio State tried to make the football coach become the athletics director to help sweeten the deal, but John Richards lasted just one season holding both roles before resigning. Wilce kept the job for 16 seasons and helped stabilize the role for the program.

2. Team manager William Dougherty wrote the lyrics and melody to "Across the Field" in 1915 and dedicated the song to coach John Wilce. The song was first performed when Ohio State faced Illinois in 1915 and is one of two official fight songs for the Buckeyes. The song replaced Ohio State's old fight song "Wahoo! Wahoo!", which was sung to the tune of "Roll, Jordan, Roll."

3. Ohio State began the capital campaign for the construction of Ohio Stadium in October 1920 with the goal of raising $600,000 for the project. By the end of November, the school had raised $923,000, and ground was broken the following August. The project took only 14 months and ended up costing north of $1.5 million, more than two-thirds of which had been pledged by supporters of the program. Many had assumed the new

stadium would have a capacity of around 35,000 fans, but the stadium opened with a capacity of more than 60,000. In 1928, the school announced it had paid back all the debt for building the stadium.

4. Perhaps the most famous band tradition in college football, the Ohio State band performs "Script Ohio" at halftime or after every Buckeye home game. The formation was first introduced in 1936 at Ohio State's game with Pittsburgh and has become one of the best traditions in college football. The honor of dotting the "i" is normally reserved for a fourth- or fifth-year sousaphone player, but there have been occasions where a special celebrity is given the honor. Many of the band's former directors have been given the honor and so have former Ohio State coaches Woody Hayes and Earle Bruce, comedian Bob Hope, astronaut and U.S. Senator John Glenn, golfer Jack Nicklaus, and boxer Buster Douglas.

5. In 1934, Ohio State coach Francis Schmidt was asked how the Buckeyes would perform against Michigan, and he quipped, "They put their pants on one leg at a time just like everybody else." Ohio State shut out the Wolverines four consecutive years under Schmidt's leadership, and the Gold Pants Club was born. Now every player who beats Michigan earns a golden pants charm to honor the victory over their bitter rivals. After the 2020 meeting was canceled, the Buckeyes have won eight straight over the Wolverines and captured 17 of the last 19 meetings between the schools.

6. If you look at the southwest corner of Ohio Stadium, you will see rows of buckeye trees, planted to honor each of the Buckeyes' All-Americans. The tradition of Buckeye Grove began in 1934 and has been carried on as a way to honor the many great players who have worn the scarlet and gray over the years.

7. The first night game at "The Horseshoe" was a thriller between Ohio State and Pittsburgh. The visiting Panthers held a 7-3 lead late in the fourth quarter and had forced the Buckeyes into a fourth-and-goal at the 2-yard line. The run-oriented Buckeyes lined up as if to run the ball, but Jim Karsatos shocked everyone by throwing the winning touchdown pass to Cris Carter for the win. The Buckeyes are 16-5 at home in games that start at 5:00 p.m. or later.

8. Ohio State has been involved in several interesting games over the years. In 1912, John Richards pulled his team off the field with five minutes left against Penn State because of excessively rough play. The Buckeyes were trailing 37-0 at the time, but the score is officially a 1-0 forfeit loss. In 1943, Ohio State and Illinois were tied at 26 at the end of regulation, and both teams assumed the game ended in a tie. However, the Fighting Illini had been called for a penalty on the final play of the game, so 20 minutes later the teams were called back onto the field, and John Stungis kicked the game-winning 27-yard field goal.

9. Ohio State has 33 former players and head coaches in the College Football Hall of Fame. The first people inducted

were running back Chic Harley and coach Howard Jones in 1951. Keith Byars was the latest to be inducted, as a member of the class of 2020.

10. Three times in Ohio State's history, the Buckeyes have gone undefeated and untied without winning the national championship. In 1916, there was no poll or governing body to determine a national champion, so the Buckeyes went 7-0 without any official title. Ohio State wasn't even Big Ten champions that year because the conference did not officially recognize championships from the early years until much later. In 2012, Ohio State was barred from the postseason due to the infractions committed that vacated the 2010 season, but the Buckeyes still won all 12 games that year even if they could not be officially deemed conference or national champions.

CHAPTER 2:

NUMBERS GAME

QUIZ TIME!

1. Archie Griffin's number 45 was the first number ever retired at Ohio State in any sport.

    a. True
    b. False

2. Which of these former players did NOT wear the superstitious number 13 for the Buckeyes?

    a. Kenny Guiton
    b. Maurice Clarett
    c. Eli Apple
    d. Cardale Jones

3. What number was NOT worn by an Ohio State player who is currently enshrined in the Pro Football Hall of Fame?

    a. 42
    b. 44
    c. 57
    d. 75

4. Which of these famous Buckeyes did NOT wear number 4 during his time in Columbus?

   a. Santonio Holmes
   b. Kirk Herbstreit
   c. DeVier Posey
   d. Kurt Coleman

5. What number did Cris Carter wear during his three years at Ohio State?

   a. 2
   b. 3
   c. 7
   d. 22

6. Which number did the Bosa brothers wear while terrorizing opposing backfields for Ohio State?

   a. 94
   b. 96
   c. 97
   d. 98

7. Ohio State has retired the jersey numbers only of Heisman Trophy winners.

   a. True
   b. False

8. Ohio State's first Heisman Trophy winner, Les Horvath, wore three different numbers during his time in Columbus. Which was NOT one of them?

   a. 6
   b. 22

c. 48

d. 53

9. Who was the last person to wear number 27 for Ohio State before the school retired that uniform in honor of Eddie George?

    a. Clarence Royal

    b. Michael Willis

    c. Eddie George

    d. Jerry Westbrooks

10. Which of these numbers was NOT worn by one of Ohio State's Heisman Trophy winners?

    a. 10

    b. 31

    c. 34

    d. 40

11. Which of these receivers wore the same number as Terry Glenn during their Ohio State career?

    a. Brian Hartline

    b. Chris Olave

    c. Noah Brown

    d. Terry McLaurin

12. What number did Dane Sanzenbacher wear while carving up defenses for the Buckeyes?

    a. 2

    b. 12

    c. 22

    d. 82

13. Ohio State's only Lou Groza Award winner wore a single-digit number.

    a. True

    b. False

14. What number did Andy Katzenmoyer wear while wreaking havoc for the Buckeyes?

    a. 33

    b. 42

    c. 45

    d. 47

15. Which now-retired number did Ohio State interim coach Luke Fickell wear during his Buckeyes career?

    a. 22

    b. 31

    c. 45

    d. 99

16. Which number did Joey Galloway wear as a freshman in 1990?

    a. 5

    b. 27

    c. 36

    d. 87

17. What number did Chris Spielman wear at Ohio State?

    a. 54

    b. 48

    c. 44

    d. 36

18. What number was NOT worn by one of Ohio State's three winners of the Rimington Trophy?

    a. 54
    b. 65
    c. 55
    d. 68

19. Ohio State's school colors of scarlet and gray predate the football program.

    a. True
    b. False

20. What color are the buckeye decals given out to players during the season for big plays and consistency?

    a. Black
    b. Green
    c. White
    d. Scarlet

QUIZ ANSWERS

1. A – True

2. D – Cardale Jones

3. C – 57

4. C – DeVier Posey

5. A – 2

6. C – 97

7. B – False

8. A – 6

9. D – Jerry Westbrooks

10. C – 34

11. D – Terry McLaurin

12. B – 12

13. B – False

14. C – 45

15. D – 99

16. B – 27

17. D – 36

18. C – 55

19. A – True

20. B – Green

DID YOU KNOW?

1. Nearly two decades before the Buckeyes took to the gridiron for the first time, Ohio State selected scarlet and gray as the school's official colors. In 1878, a group of three students met to decide on the official school colors and chose scarlet and gray. One committee member said it was a "pleasing combination" and noted that no other school in the country had adopted those colors.

2. The famous stickers of buckeye leaves first began to appear on helmets in 1968 at the suggestion of athletic trainer Ernie Biggs. The exact reason behind the sudden switch that year is lost to history, but the consensus is that the stickers provided that extra bit of motivation for the Buckeyes players. Woody Hayes doled out the stickers for big plays and consistent play on the field, and the reward of a sticker was said to motivate the players to perform better. The stickers have been tweaked over the years and are now about the size of a quarter and feature a green buckeye leaf. Every coaching staff has a different vision for how stickers are earned, but Jim Tressel used to award them to units more than to individuals. Everyone received a sticker for a win, and two if it was a Big Ten win, and each unit would receive one for certain benchmarks like explosive plays or three-and-outs.

3. Ohio State did not retire a single number in any sport until 1999 when the administration surprised Archie

Griffin by retiring his number 45 at halftime of the Buckeyes' game with Iowa on October 30. Despite being a prominent figure within the athletics department at the time, Griffin did not know about the ceremony, which began the department's goal of retiring the number of all five Heisman Trophy winners before renovations of Ohio Stadium were finished in 2001. Vic Janowicz and Howard Cassady had their numbers retired in 2000; Eddie George and Les Horvath had their numbers retired the following year.

4. There are only two non-winners of the Heisman Trophy to have their jerseys retired by Ohio State. In 2004, Chic Harley, the Buckeyes' first three-time All-American, had his jersey retired, and defensive lineman Bill Willis's number 99 was taken out of circulation in 2007. The announcement that Harley's number will be retired was a chance to teach the younger generation of Buckeyes fans about the great running back, who was a first-team selection for the Associated Press All-Star college football team for the first half of the twentieth century ahead of Red Grange. Willis is the only defensive player to be honored with a jersey retirement. He was told about the honor on his 86th birthday.

5. When it came time for the Buckeyes to honor Troy Smith's number 10 in 2014, the department changed course about how it would "retire" numbers. Smith's number 10 is officially enshrined at Ohio Stadium to honor his Heisman Trophy victory, but it is not taken out of

circulation like the previous 18 numbers across all sports at Ohio State.

6. Eddie George was the best-known Buckeyes player to wear number 27, but the number was worn by another Ohio State great just two years before George's arrival on campus. For his first season in Columbus, Joey Galloway wore number 27 and caught 14 passes for 255 yards and a touchdown in that uniform number. It was worn by running back Troy Lopes and defensive back Girmar Johnson in 1991 before George took the number in 1992 and turned it into a legendary uniform for the Buckeyes.

7. Mike Nugent originally was going to wear number 47 when he arrived in Columbus because he was a friend of Ohio State's outgoing kicker, Dan Stultz, who wore the jersey. However, a position change forced another player to wear number 47, and Nugent was assigned number 85 instead. He admitted to being a little confused by the unorthodox number at first but added, "I like to think that the number doesn't make the player, the player makes the number. And hopefully I kind of got a name for myself with it like that."

8. If you're going to wear the jersey of a legend, you need to be able to live up to the prestige of the number. Andy Katzenmoyer certainly did more than enough during his Ohio State career to silence the critics, who were annoyed that he asked to wear Archie Griffin's historic number 45 for the Buckeyes. He was the Big Ten Freshman of the

Year in 1996 and was a first-team All-Big Ten linebacker all three years on campus. He had only requested number 45 because his high school number, 44, was already taken, but he turned that pressure into being one of the most successful linebackers in Ohio State history.

9. The Bosa brothers took the legacy of their father's number 97 to a whole new level during their combined six years in Columbus. Between 2013 and 2018, one of the two Bosa brothers was wearing number 97 for Ohio State and creating mayhem in the backfield for opponents. John Bosa wore number 97 for five years in the NFL with the Miami Dolphins, and his sons, Joey and Nick, have worn it every stop along the way in their college football careers.

10. Before the 2020 season, the NCAA allowed teams to hand out a jersey number 0, and Ohio State used it as a chance to honor one of its greats. The number will be awarded to the player who best embodies the toughness, accountability, and fight of former Buckeyes great Bill Willis. In a statement announcing Jonathan Cooper as the inaugural honoree, Ohio State wrote "the number '0' is a badge of honor. It represents fight—the backbone of our culture." The Buckeyes call the jersey "Block O."

CHAPTER 3:

CALLING THE SIGNALS

QUIZ TIME!

1. Cardale Jones easily holds the record for most wins without a loss as an Ohio State starting quarterback, with how many victories?

   a. 9

   b. 11

   c. 13

   d. 14

2. Which of these quarterbacks did NOT win 30 games as the Buckeyes' starter?

   a. J.T. Barrett

   b. Cornelius Greene

   c. Braxton Miller

   d. Bobby Hoying

3. Who was Ohio State's starting quarterback in the final tie in Buckeyes history?

   a. Kirk Herbstreit

   b. Bobby Hoying

c. Greg Frey

d. Stanley Jackson

4. Every quarterback to have started a game for Ohio State since at least 1960 has won at least one game.

a. True

b. False

5. How many Ohio State quarterbacks have thrown for 5,000 yards in their careers in Columbus?

a. 9

b. 10

c. 11

d. 12

6. Who was the first quarterback in Ohio State history to throw for 3,000 yards in a season?

a. Joe Germaine

b. Art Schlichter

c. Craig Krenzel

d. Bobby Hoying

7. Which of these quarterback pairs never both threw for 100 yards in the same game?

a. Dwayne Haskins and J.T. Barrett

b. Joe Bauserman and Braxton Miller

c. Steve Bellisari and Craig Krenzel

d. Bobby Hoying and Bret Powers

8. Dwayne Haskins threw for 400 yards in the same number of games that he threw for less than 300 yards.

a. True

b. False

9. Whose single-season record did Dwayne Haskins break in 2018 by throwing for 300 yards in nine different games?

   a. Braxton Miller

   b. J.T. Barrett

   c. Troy Smith

   d. Joe Germaine

10. Who threw the longest pass in Ohio State history, a 90-yard touchdown connection?

   a. Troy Smith

   b. J.T. Barrett

   c. Kenny Guiton

   d. Greg Frey

11. Dwayne Haskins is responsible for all but one of the 400-yard passing performances in Ohio State history. Who is responsible for the other one?

   a. Troy Smith

   b. J.T. Barrett

   c. Art Schlichter

   d. Cardale Jones

12. What is the Ohio State record for most passes in a game without throwing an interception?

   a. 45

   b. 49

   c. 52

   d. 54

13. Only two quarterbacks have completed 500 passes in their Ohio State careers.

    a. True
    b. False

14. J.T. Barrett broke the record for most consecutive completions in a game with how many against Penn State in 2017?

    a. 13
    b. 14
    c. 15
    d. 16

15. How many times did Braxton Miller run for 100 yards in a game?

    a. 12
    b. 14
    c. 16
    d. 18

16. Before Ohio State quarterback Joe Burrow's Heisman Trophy victory in 2019, Troy Smith held the record for the highest percentage of points earned.

    a. True
    b. False

17. Which school intercepted Art Schlichter five times in 1978 to set the single-game record for most interceptions thrown by an Ohio State quarterback?

    a. Purdue
    b. Penn State

c. Wisconsin

d. Iowa

18. Who was the first quarterback to throw five touchdowns in a game for the Buckeyes?

   a. Todd Boeckman

   b. J.T. Barrett

   c. Bobby Hoying

   d. John Borton

19. Which of these Ohio State quarterbacks did NOT win the *Chicago Tribune*'s Silver Football Award as the Big Ten MVP?

   a. Terrelle Pryor

   b. Art Schlichter

   c. Joe Germaine

   d. Cornelius Greene

20. When was the first time Ohio State had 1,000-yard passers in consecutive seasons?

   a. 1965-66

   b. 1969-70

   c. 1974-75

   d. 1977-78

QUIZ ANSWERS

1. B – 11

2. C – Braxton Miller

3. B – Bobby Hoying

4. A – True

5. D – 12

6. D – Bobby Hoying

7. C – Steve Bellisari and Craig Krenzel

8. A – True

9. D – Joe Germaine

10. C – Kenny Guiton

11. C – Art Schlichter

12. C – 52

13. B – False

14. D – 16

15. B – 14

16. A – True

17. B – Penn State

18. D – John Borton

19. A – Terrelle Pryor

20. A – 1965-66

DID YOU KNOW?

1. Cornelius Greene was Ohio State's first black starting quarterback, and that wasn't a popular decision when Woody Hayes made it in 1973. Greene received 50 letters per week from the Ku Klux Klan and other racist organizations, and he received numerous death threats on the phone in the dorm room that he shared with Archie Griffin. The pressure ceased when Greene led the Buckeyes to a 56-7 win over Minnesota in the season opener, the first of 33 wins Greene had as Ohio State's starting quarterback. Greene finished his Ohio State career with more than 2,000 passing and rushing yards and was the 1975 recipient of the *Chicago Tribune* Silver Football as Big Ten MVP.

2. Art Schlichter is the quarterback who changed the future of Ohio State's offense. George Chaump was hired on as an offensive assistant in 1968, and he was the first Buckeyes coach to lay eyes on Schlichter in high school at nearby Miami Trace. After showing Woody Hayes several reels of film on the quarterback, Chaump was able to get Hayes to a game, and the head coach was sold. Schlichter was set to commit to Michigan, but Hayes promised the young quarterback that he would start as a freshman and that the Buckeyes would open up the offense. That promise came a day before Michigan coach Bo Schembechler was scheduled to meet the Schlichters at their house, and when

Art's father told Schembechler about Hayes's promise, he stormed out in anger, claiming Hayes would not hold his promises to the family.

3. Most people likely remember Tom Tupa as a punter because that is ultimately what earned him the most publicity. He was a three-time first-team All-Big Ten punter with the Buckeyes, but he was also the team's starting quarterback in 1987 and was almost solely a quarterback for his first five seasons in the NFL. Tupa threw for 1,786 yards in his only season as the starter in Columbus and completed 55.4% of his passes that season, while tossing 12 touchdown passes.

4. Kirk Herbstreit was unremarkable as Ohio State's starter in 1992, but he has become one of the preeminent faces of college football through his role at ESPN. However, Herbstreit almost passed on the opportunity to get into the media business out of college in 1993. He was all set to take a corporate sales job with an $85,000 base salary and all the perks of the corporate life when the Columbus radio station offered him $12,000 and none of the benefits to do an afternoon talk show and the sideline reports for Ohio State football games. Two years later, ESPN2 hired him as a sideline reporter, and he eventually moved into the booth to broadcast Arena Football League games in 1996. Less than a year later, ESPN hired Herbstreit to replace Craig James on *College Gameday*.

5. Bobby Hoying comes from a very athletic family. His grandfather, Wally Post, played 15 seasons of professional

baseball for the Cincinnati Reds and Cleveland Indians, hitting 210 home runs and collecting just under 700 RBI in his career. Hoying left Ohio State after four years as the school's record-holder in touchdown passes and completion percentage, and he ranked second in passing yards. He also became the first Big Ten athlete to win the William V. Campbell Trophy, known as the academic Heisman, as a senior in 1995.

6. Craig Krenzel wasn't on the road to being a Big Ten starting quarterback until the summer before his freshman year in high school. He was throwing a football in the gym that summer when Ford High's new football coach, Terry Copacia, spotted him. He was intrigued by Krenzel's potential and worked with him for more than a year on his throwing motion. Copacia wanted to start Krenzel as a sophomore but went with the senior quarterback instead until Ford fell behind in the opening game of the season. Krenzel came in and brought his team to within range of a winning field goal that missed. By the end of the season, Krenzel was the starter, and Copacia started shopping his highlight tape to the college coaches he knew. Many of the smaller schools passed on Krenzel, assuming the bigger schools would come calling. Michigan State and Boston College were his biggest pursuers before he visited Ohio State as a junior and decided to commit to the Buckeyes.

7. Troy Smith's 2006 season was so good that he was a clear runaway winner of the Heisman Trophy. After throwing for 2,542 yards and 30 touchdowns as a senior, 801 of the

924 voters for the 2006 Heisman put Smith's name on the top line as the winner. Before Joe Burrow winning in 2019, Smith accumulated the highest proportion of points with 91.63%. Smith also had the second-largest margin of victory before Burrow's victory knocked him to third.

8. In September 2020, Cardale Jones tweeted that he was in the process of writing a book about his career at Ohio State. He certainly has a lot of good fodder to write about his four years in Columbus. Jones first came to national prominence for tweeting, "Why should we have to go to class if we came here to play FOOTBALL, we ain't come to play SCHOOL, classes are POINTLESS," as a freshman. As a redshirt sophomore, he was thrust into game action after Braxton Miller and J.T. Barrett were injured, and he led the Buckeyes to wins in the Big Ten championship game, the national semifinals, and the national championship game during the 2014 season. Jones opted to return to school for the 2015 campaign and eventually earned the starting quarterback job, but it was a struggle that affected his draft stock.

9. When J.T. Barrett left the field after the 2017 Cotton Bowl, he took with him 39 school or Big Ten records, concluding the greatest statistical career for an Ohio State quarterback. His 104 passing touchdowns are a Big Ten record as are his more than 12,600 yards of total offense. He won a school-record 38 games, completed 63.5% of his passes, threw for 300 yards eight times, and gained more than 200 yards of offense in 37 games. He also holds the

Ohio State record for a quarterback with 3,263 career rushing yards.

10. If Barrett had the greatest statistical career of an Ohio State quarterback, Dwayne Haskins had the greatest season in Buckeyes history in 2018. He threw for 400 yards in five of the 14 games he started that season, and he fell four yards shy of a sixth 400-yard performance as well. His nine 300-yard games in 2018 not only set the single-season record but also set the career record at Ohio State. His school-record 4,831 yards that season ranks 11th in school history for career passing yards, and he is the only Ohio State quarterback to throw for at least 200 yards in every game of the season. He completed a Big Ten record 373 passes for a school-record 70% completion percentage.

CHAPTER 4:

BETWEEN THE TACKLES

QUIZ TIME!

1. Who is the only Ohio State running back to lead the Buckeyes in rushing for four consecutive seasons?

    a. J.K. Dobbins

    b. Bob Ferguson

    c. Eddie George

    d. Archie Griffin

2. Who was the first Ohio State running back to rush for 1,000 yards in a season?

    a. Archie Griffin

    b. Bob Ferguson

    c. John Brockington

    d. Jim Otis

3. How many times has an Ohio State player rushed for 200 yards in a game?

    a. 19

    b. 23

c. 26

d. 29

4. Who was the first Ohio State player to rush for 200 yards in a single game?

a. Loren White

b. Oliver Cline

c. Calvin Murray

d. Archie Griffin

5. Eddie George and Ezekiel Elliott are tied in the record books with the most 200-yard games for the Buckeyes, with how many?

a. 5

b. 4

c. 3

d. 2

6. Eddie George ran for 4,000 yards in his Ohio State career.

a. True

b. False

7. Which running back did NOT average 100 yards per game for his Ohio State career?

a. Archie Griffin

b. J.K. Dobbins

c. Eddie George

d. Ezekiel Elliott

8. The same player holds the Ohio State record for most rushing touchdowns in a season and a career.

a. True

b. False

9. Who did NOT rush for 100 yards against Indiana in 2011, the last time Ohio State had three 100-yard rushers in the same game?

a. Braxton Miller

b. Carlos Hyde

c. Dan Heron

d. Jordan Hall

10. In which year did an Ohio State running back NOT win the Heisman Trophy?

a. 1944

b. 1949

c. 1950

d. 1955

11. How many times did Archie Griffin NOT rush for 100 yards in a game during his Ohio State career?

a. 12

b. 14

c. 16

d. 18

12. Archie Griffin had more rushing yards and touchdowns as a sophomore in 1973 than he did in his Heisman-winning campaign of 1975.

a. True

b. False

13. What was Les Horvath's career high for rushing yards in a game, set during his Heisman-winning 1944 season?

    a. 114 yards
    b. 128 yards
    c. 141 yards
    d. 157 yards

14. Like most players of the era, Vic Janowicz was a do-everything back for the Buckeyes in his career, including kicking. How long was his famous field goal in the "Snow Bowl" against Michigan in 1950 for Ohio State's only points in the game?

    a. 21 yards
    b. 24 yards
    c. 27 yards
    d. 30 yards

15. How many touchdowns did Howard Cassady score in his first game for the Buckeyes?

    a. 0
    b. 1
    c. 2
    d. 3

16. Which of these Ohio State running backs was NOT the Big Ten Freshman of the Year?

    a. Mike Weber
    b. Ezekiel Elliott
    c. Maurice Clarett
    d. Robert Smith

17. Which of these Ohio State running backs was NOT a three-time first-team All-American?

   a. Lew Hinchman
   b. Howard Cassady
   c. Chic Harley
   d. Archie Griffin

18. How many yards did J.K. Dobbins rush for in 2019 to become Ohio State's first single-season 2,000-yard rusher?

   a. 2,159 yards
   b. 2,124 yards
   c. 2,097 yards
   d. 2,003 yards

19. Trey Sermon became the first Ohio State player to rush for 300 yards in a game during the 2020 Big Ten championship game against Northwestern.

   a. True
   b. False

20. Who did NOT win the Maxwell Award during his time at Ohio State?

   a. Howard Cassady
   b. Bob Ferguson
   c. Les Horvath
   d. Eddie George

QUIZ ANSWERS

1. D – Archie Griffin

2. D – Jim Otis

3. C – 26

4. B – Oliver Cline

5. A – 5

6. B – False

7. C – Eddie George

8. A – True

9. D – Jordan Hall

10. B – 1949

11. A – 12

12. A – True

13. C – 141 yards

14. C – 27 yards

15. D – 3

16. B – Ezekiel Elliott

17. B – Howard Cassady

18. D – 2,003 yards

19. B – False

20. C – Les Horvath

DID YOU KNOW?

1. Chic Harley was the original Ohio State superstar when he became the program's first three-time All-American from 1916 to 1919. Harley skipped the 1918 season to join the military and fight in World War I but returned to the Buckeyes in 1919 and again dominated the competition. The popularity of Harley helped lift the profile of Ohio State's football program and was a catalyst behind the construction of Ohio Stadium. Some still refer to the stadium as the "House that Harley Built" because of his influence on the early days of the Buckeyes.

2. Les Horvath's Heisman Trophy-winning season wasn't supposed to happen. Horvath was scheduled to ride off into retirement from football after helping the Buckeyes win the national title in 1942, and he entered dental school in 1943. But, because of the player shortage in 1944 caused by World War II, the NCAA made freshmen eligible and granted an extra year to those who had previously been ineligible as freshmen. Carroll Widdoes convinced Horvath to return for one last season while he was in dental school by telling him he wouldn't have to practice, and the school would fly him to games so he could have more time to study. Horvath went on to become Ohio State's first Heisman winner thanks to the NCAA rule change after rushing for 924 yards and 12 touchdowns for the Buckeyes in 1944.

3. Vic Janowicz was a do-it-all back for the Buckeyes, who won the Heisman Trophy as a junior in 1950. In his award-winning season, Janowicz was the kicker, punter, quarterback, and running back for the Buckeyes. He led the team with 314 rushing yards and 561 passing yards in 1950, but he could not replicate that success in 1951. Janowicz went on to play professional baseball for two years after graduation despite not playing for the Buckeyes but was drafted into the NFL after he struggled to play baseball at the pro level.

4. Howard Cassady made an instant impact in his first game as a Buckeyes player in 1952. He scored three of his four touchdowns of the season in the opener when he came off the bench to help Ohio State beat Indiana. He was a first-team All-American in 1954, helping to lead the Buckeyes to a perfect 10-0 record, but that was just a preview of what would come the following year. Cassady ran for 958 yards and 15 touchdowns in 1955 to earn the Heisman Trophy and be named the Associated Press Athlete of the Year. He is the first Heisman winner to earn more than 2,000 votes in the voting.

5. Archie Griffin is the only two-time Heisman Trophy winner, but he wasn't even the Big Ten's Most Valuable Player when he won his second Heisman in 1975. Griffin was awarded the *Chicago Tribune*'s Silver Football in 1973 and 1974, but Buckeyes quarterback Cornelius Greene won the award in 1975. Griffin was likely bound to win the award again, but the panel could only vote for those

who were voted their own team's MVP, and Greene was Ohio State's choice. It was Griffin's politicking that helped Greene win the award that season, telling teammates, "Look, I won that award in '73. I won that award in '74. You guys got to vote for Corny. He deserves to win it." Still, Greene only won the team MVP award by one vote—Griffin's.

6. When Eddie George was being recruited to play college football, most of the schools who wanted George's talent were planning to convert him to linebacker. Ohio State was willing to give George a chance as a running back, and the Buckeyes never regretted that decision. The fans, though, were not as kind to George after he fumbled twice inside the 5-yard line against Illinois as a true freshman. Many had told George he should transfer, and he would never make it as a running back at Ohio State. Three years later, he set a major record against the Fighting Illini en route to what was then a school-record 1,927 yards and fell one shy of the Buckeyes' single-season record with 24 touchdowns. George took home every major award for running backs in 1995: the Heisman Trophy, the Doak Walker Award, the Maxwell Award, and the Walter Camp Award.

7. Three of the four Ohio State players to win the Maxwell Award as the best player in college football also won the Heisman Trophy. The exception is Bob Ferguson, who in 1961 was the runner-up for the Heisman but did win the Maxwell Award. A two-time unanimous All-American

for the Buckeyes, he ran for 938 yards and 11 touchdowns during his senior year in 1961. Ernie Davis beat out Ferguson for the Heisman that year by just 53 points, the third-smallest margin of victory in the history of the award.

8. Ohio State fans have Archie Griffin to thank for Keith Byars choosing the Buckeyes over Pittsburgh. Byars was deciding between Ohio State and Pittsburgh when he met Griffin on the Bengals' practice field in the summer of 1981. All Griffin had to say was that Byars should join the pantheon of great Ohio high school running backs to suit up for the Scarlet and Gray, and Byars made his decision. Of course, Byars would have been stuck at tight end in high school if not for a whim from an assistant coach when Byars was a sophomore. Byars was put in at running back almost as a joke by an assistant coach, and Byars knew that if he scored on the first-team defense he wouldn't have to run sprints. So he bulldozed the unit a few times in that practice, and he was a running back as a junior and senior, setting up that fateful meeting with Griffin in 1981.

9. Maurice Clarett is the greatest what-if story in Ohio State history. He was the 2002 Big Ten Freshman of the Year and a first-team all-conference selection that season while leading the Buckeyes to the national championship. He ran for two touchdowns in the title game against Miami, including the winning score in the second overtime from five yards out. But Clarett never saw the field again for

the Buckeyes after that night in Arizona. By the following July, he was ruled ineligible and suspended for the entire 2003 season for accepting impermissible benefits. He tried to sue the NFL to be eligible for the 2004 Draft, but he lost the case in court and had to wait until 2005 to be drafted. He ran for 1,237 yards and 16 touchdowns in his only season in Columbus. Had he played all four years at Ohio State and averaged the same production for the next three years, he would have been about 600 yards shy of Archie Griffin's school record and would have obliterated the record for rushing touchdowns.

10. Ezekiel Elliott has never been a fan of shirts. The running back is known for tucking his jersey under his shoulder pads to show off his midsection, which he did consistently at Ohio State before the NCAA banned the look. He even showed up to class one day in high school with just a blazer on. There was an issue when Elliott tried to remove the blazer during class, prompting one of his football coaches to require him to wear a shirt to class. As a sophomore and junior, though, Elliott was nearly untouchable on the field, rushing for 1,800 yards in consecutive seasons and finishing with 41 touchdowns in those two years. He and Eddie George are the only players to rush for 200 yards in a game three times in one season and five times in a career.

CHAPTER 5:

CATCHING THE BALL

QUIZ TIME!

1. Who holds the Ohio State record for most receptions in a career?

    a. Terry Glenn
    b. David Boston
    c. Cris Carter
    d. K.J. Hill

2. Only five Ohio State receivers have gone over 1,000 receiving yards in a season.

    a. True
    b. False

3. How many receptions did David Boston have in 1997 against Penn State to set the Buckeyes' record for most catches in a game?

    a. 13
    b. 14
    c. 15
    d. 16

4. Which of these Buckeyes receivers did NOT eclipse 2,500 yards in their Ohio State careers?

   a. Michael Jenkins
   b. Joey Galloway
   c. Gary Williams
   d. Cris Carter

5. Who is one of the four players tied for the school record with four touchdown catches in a game?

   a. Noah Brown
   b. David Boston
   c. Joey Galloway
   d. Santonio Holmes

6. Despite the abridged season, Ohio State had three games in which two receivers had at least 100 yards, tying the record for the most occurrences in a season that the Buckeyes set in which year?

   a. 2018
   b. 1998
   c. 1980
   d. 1969

7. Which tight end holds the Ohio State career records for receptions and receiving yards by a tight end?

   a. Billy Anders
   b. Bob Grimes
   c. John Frank
   d. Bruce Jankowski

8. Dick LeBeau led the Buckeyes in catches in two consecutive seasons during his Ohio State career.

    a. True

    b. False

9. Who was the first player to lead the Buckeyes in receiving in three consecutive seasons?

    a. David Boston

    b. Doug Donley

    c. Gary Williams

    d. Charles Bryant

10. Who holds the Ohio State record with five straight games of at least 100 receiving yards?

    a. Michael Thomas

    b. Terry Glenn

    c. David Boston

    d. Cris Carter

11. Gary Williams was the first Ohio State receiver to accomplish which feat?

    a. Go over 1,000 yards in a season

    b. Catch 50 passes in a season

    c. Score 10 touchdowns in a season

    d. Be named a first-team All-American

12. Cris Carter became Ohio State's first receiver to be named an All-American in which season?

    a. 1984

    b. 1985

c. 1986

d. 1987

13. No Ohio State receiver has ever won the Biletnikoff Award for the best wide receiver in the country.

    a. True

    b. False

14. Who did Ohio State play in 1995 when Terry Glenn set the school record for receiving yards in a game?

    a. Youngstown State

    b. Purdue

    c. Indiana

    d. Pittsburgh

15. How many records did David Boston set or tie during his three seasons in Columbus?

    a. 12

    b. 10

    c. 8

    d. 7

16. How many yards did Michael Jenkins have in his Ohio State career to set the school record?

    a. 2,898

    b. 2,784

    c. 2,652

    d. 2,541

17. Though listed as a wide receiver, Ted Ginn Jr. probably made his largest contributions on special teams. How

many return touchdowns did the speedster have in his career?

a. 6
b. 7
c. 8
d. 9

18. Despite not ranking in the top 10 for either career receptions or career receiving yards for a tight end, Jake Stoneburner holds the Ohio State record for career touchdown catches by a tight end, with how many?

a. 7
b. 9
c. 11
d. 13

19. Ohio State has NOT had a receiver with 200 receiving yards in a game in the twenty-first century.

a. True
b. False

20. Who is the only receiver in the last 25 years to lead Ohio State in scoring?

c. Santonio Holmes
d. David Boston
e. Parris Campbell
f. Michael Thomas

QUIZ ANSWERS

1. D – K.J. Hill

2. A – True

3. B – 14

4. B – Joey Galloway

5. A – Noah Brown

6. C – 1980

7. C – John Frank

8. A – True

9. D – Charles Bryant

10. D – Cris Carter

11. B – Catch 50 passes in a season

12. C – 1986

13. B – False

14. D – Pittsburgh

15. A – 12

16. A – 2,898

17. C – 8

18. D – 13

19. B – False

20. C – Parris Campbell

DID YOU KNOW?

1. Paul Warfield was mostly a running back in Woody Hayes's wing-T system, but he did lead the Buckeyes in receptions in 1962 and 1963. Warfield's lasting memory of Ohio State wasn't something that happened on the field, though. Warfield was part of the Buckeyes team that had traveled to play Michigan the day John F. Kennedy was assassinated, and "The Game" was postponed a week due to national mourning. Warfield said he remembers the team was very anxious about the future of the country in light of the tragedy, and Hayes delivered a lecture about the U.S. government and the strengths and weaknesses of Lyndon Johnson that Warfield said kept the team at ease.

2. John Frank faced a dilemma on September 17, 1983, as number six Ohio State traveled to face number two Oklahoma. The Buckeyes tight end is Jewish, and the primetime game against the Sooners fell on Yom Kippur, the holiest day of the year in Judaism, so Frank was unsure if he would play. He ended up going to synagogue in Oklahoma City on Friday night before the game, then played the next day, catching two touchdown passes in the Buckeyes' win. Frank caught just four touchdowns the entire 1983 season, but his two scores helped stake Ohio State to a 14-0 lead that it then rode to victory.

3. Doug Donley is proof of the tremendous effect Woody Hayes can have on young football players in Ohio. The day Hayes came to visit Donley's home, the coach stopped by Donley's basketball practice first, and his mere presence caused the team to have one of its more intense practices of the season. Then, when Hayes was in Donley's home, Michigan coach Bo Schembechler called, and Donley's mother had him take the call in a bedroom. When he returned to the dinner table, Hayes asked who was on the phone and, when he heard it was Schembechler, asked Donley for his verbal commitment right then and there. Too nervous to turn down Hayes at the moment, Donley shook the coach's hand and made the decision to play at Ohio State.

4. Cris Carter set a lot of records during his career at Ohio State, but it was the way it ended that left a sour taste in many people's mouths. Carter was ruled ineligible for the 1987 season when it was discovered that he accepted money from two different sports agents. He eventually pled guilty to defrauding Ohio State over the issue, but after being ruled ineligible for 1987, Carter applied to be part of the NFL Supplemental Draft that season. He was selected by the Philadelphia Eagles in the 1987 Supplemental Draft, beginning his Hall of Fame pro career.

5. Terry Glenn's path to Ohio State as a walk-on receiver was filled with tragedy and heartbreak. His father abandoned the family when he was young, and his mother was beaten to death when he was 13 years old. He

bounced around to four different houses within the first year after his mother's death, eventually living with the Henley family, whose son, June, was a friend of Glenn's cousin. Glenn admitted in a *Chicago Tribune* article that he contemplated suicide after his mother's death, but that he knew he had to live for his younger sister, Dorothy, who was seven at the time. Once at Ohio State, a computer error kept him eligible as a sophomore, setting the scene for a remarkable 1995 season when he won the Biletnikoff Award as the nation's best receiver.

6. Only 19 times in Ohio State history has a player caught 10 or more passes in a game, and David Boston had five of those performances. In 1996, he tied Gary Williams's record with 13 catches against Indiana, and the following year, he broke the record with 14 receptions against Penn State. Boston only gained 153 yards and scored once in that loss to the Nittany Lions, though. The game most people tend to remember Boston for was his 10 catches for 217 yards and two touchdowns in a win over Michigan the following year, the only 200-yard performance of Boston's Ohio State career.

7. In an interview on the Atlanta Falcons' podcast, *Bird Noises*, Michael Jenkins admitted that he ran the wrong route on the famous "Holy Buckeye" play against Purdue. Jenkins said he believes he was supposed to run a post on the play, but instead, he ran a go route and caught the game-winning 37-yard touchdown pass to keep Ohio State's perfect season alive. The strange part about that

catch is that the cornerback covering Jenkins on the play was Antwaun Rogers, who played youth football with Jenkins, and the two are still friends and talk.

8. Ted Ginn Jr. came very close to throwing a pass from the "Shot Ginn" formation in the 2004 Alamo Bowl. After Justin Zwick, replacing a suspended Troy Smith, tweaked his leg, the Buckeyes decided to let Ginn play quarterback instead of burning the redshirt of Todd Boeckman. Ohio State only called running plays with Ginn in at quarterback, but they had a passing play dialed up until the play clock ran short and forced an audible into a running play. Ginn caught six passes for 78 yards and ran eight times for 40 yards and a score to be named the game's MVP as Ohio State won 33-7.

9. Michael Thomas comes from excellent receiving bloodlines thanks to his uncle, Keyshawn Johnson, a standout at Southern California who was the 1st overall pick in the 1996 NFL Draft. Perhaps motivated by his uncle's success, Thomas made an instant impact at Ohio State by catching 12 passes for 131 yards in Ohio State's spring game in 2012 before he even played a college snap. He played sparingly as a freshman before redshirting his sophomore year, and then he broke out as a junior and senior, leading the Buckeyes in receptions and receiving yards both seasons.

10. Before K.J. Hill broke David Boston's record for career receptions, he had to commit to Ohio State. That was a

very interesting ordeal for Hill, who ended up getting into a fight with the coaching staff at Arkansas, where he lived. Hill took to Twitter to confirm a "crazy but true" story on former Ohio State receivers coach Zach Smith's podcast about Hill's recruitment. According to Smith, Arkansas coach Bret Bielema called Ohio State defensive coordinator Chris Ash to tell him Hill wasn't going to be coming that weekend for an official visit. It was a strange call for an opposing coach to make. As a result, after members of the Buckeyes staff spoke with Hill's parents, the family was upset with Bielema's staff, and it solidified Hill's desire to play in Columbus.

CHAPTER 6:

TRENCH WARFARE

QUIZ TIME!

1. Which national award for linemen did Orlando Pace win twice during his Ohio State career?

   a. Rimington Trophy
   b. Outland Trophy
   c. Lombardi Award
   d. Maxwell Award

2. In what place did Orlando Pace finish in the 1996 Heisman Trophy voting?

   a. 3rd
   b. 4th
   c. 5th
   d. 6th

3. Orlando Pace was the only offensive lineman to win the *Chicago Tribune* Silver Football as Big Ten MVP from 1961 to 2020.

   a. True
   b. False

4. In addition to Orlando Pace, which other Ohio State offensive lineman won both the Lombardi Award and Outland Trophy in the same season?

    a. John Hicks
    b. Pat Elflein
    c. Korey Stringer
    d. Jim Parker

5. Which Ohio State offensive lineman was the first Buckeyes lineman to win the Outland Trophy?

    a. Ted Andrick
    b. Jim Lachey
    c. John Hicks
    d. Jim Parker

6. How many times has an Ohio State player been named the Big Ten Offensive Lineman of the Year?

    a. 7
    b. 8
    c. 9
    d. 10

7. Two years before Orlando Pace won the award, which Ohio State lineman was the first offensive lineman to be named the Big Ten Freshman of the Year?

    a. Korey Stringer
    b. Alan Kline
    c. Jack Thrush
    d. Len Hartman

8. Which Ohio State center did NOT win the Rimington Award as the best center in college football?

    a. Pat Elflein
    b. LeCharles Bentley
    c. Billy Price
    d. Nick Mangold

9. Which Ohio State offensive lineman was the first first-team All-American under Woody Hayes?

    a. Jim Parker
    b. Jim Reichenbach
    c. Robert McCullough
    d. Mike Takacs

10. Ohio State won the 2002 National Championship without a single first-team All-Big Ten offensive lineman.

    a. True
    b. False

11. Who is the only Ohio State player to win the Bednarik Award as the nation's best defensive player?

    a. Joey Bosa
    b. Chase Young
    c. A.J. Hawk
    d. James Laurinaitis

12. Which Ohio State defender was the first Buckeyes player to win the Lombardi Trophy?

    a. Pepper Johnson
    b. Chris Spielman

c. Jim Stillwagon

d. Randy Gradishar

13. Who holds the Ohio State record for most career sacks?

a. Joey Bosa

b. Will Smith

c. Chase Young

d. Mike Vrabel

14. James Laurinaitis won the Butkus Award the same season that he won the Nagurski Trophy.

a. True

b. False

15. Who was the first Ohio State player to be named the Big Ten's Defensive Player of the Year?

a. Steve Tovar

b. Jason Simmons

c. Dan Wilkinson

d. Mike Vrabel

16. Andy Katzenmoyer never won a national award in his Ohio State career.

a. True

b. False

17. Who broke Tom Cousineau's record for most career tackles at Ohio State shortly after Cousineau graduated?

a. Pepper Johnson

b. Chris Spielman

    c. Marcus Marek

    d. Alvin Washington

18. Who is NOT one of the five Buckeyes to record four sacks in a game?

    a. John Simon

    b. Jason Simmons

    c. Vernon Gholston

    d. Joey Bosa

19. How many tackles for loss did Mike Vrabel have in his Ohio State career to set the school record in the category?

    a. 63

    b. 66

    c. 68

    d. 72

20. Who was the last Ohio State defender to record 20 tackles in a game, tying a school-record with 16 solo stops against Indiana in 2013?

    a. Michael Bennett

    b. Ryan Shazier

    c. Joshua Perry

    d. C.J. Barnett

QUIZ ANSWERS

1. C – Lombardi Award

2. B – 4th

3. A – True

4. A – John Hicks

5. D – Jim Parker

6. C – 9

7. A – Korey Stringer

8. D – Nick Mangold

9. D – Mike Takacs

10. A – True

11. B – Chase Young

12. C – Jim Stillwagon

13. D – Mike Vrabel

14. B – False

15. A – Steve Tovar

16. B – False

17. C – Marcus Marek

18. D – Joey Bosa

19. B – 66

20. B – Ryan Shazier

DID YOU KNOW?

1. Orlando Pace was the reason the pancake block was invented as a statistic for offensive linemen. Ohio State created the statistic in 1996 to showcase Pace's dominance on the field, keeping track of the number of times Pace left a defender on his back due to a block. The school even sent out pancake-shaped magnets to promote Pace for the national awards, notably the Heisman Trophy. Pace ended up with 80 of those pancake blocks in 1996. He finished fourth in the Heisman voting, but he cleaned up most of the other awards. He won a second consecutive Lombardi Award in 1996 in addition to winning the Outland Trophy, *Chicago Tribune* Silver Football, and the Big Ten Offensive Player of the Year.

2. John Hicks could have made history as the first interior offensive lineman to win the Heisman Trophy in 1973. The tackle won the Lombardi Award and Outland Trophy as the best lineman in the nation and became the third lineman to finish second in Heisman voting. The Buckeyes' success might have been a big issue in Hicks beating out Penn State running back John Cappelletti. Archie Griffin and Randy Gradishar finished fifth and sixth in the voting that season, but, if all those votes had gone to Hicks, he would have narrowly edged out Cappelletti's point total. Hicks finished with 114 first-place votes, roughly half the total Cappelletti received.

3. Jim Parker was Ohio State's first winner of the Outland Trophy as the best interior lineman in the country, and he received high praise from his coach Woody Hayes. The legendary coach told fans that Parker was the best lineman he ever coached because of his work ethic and incredible athleticism. When presenting Parker for induction into the Pro Football Hall of Fame, Hayes told a story about how Parker would look up at Ohio Stadium when he reached the gates to go into the locker room and shower and ponder whether he was better today than he was yesterday. If the answer was no, Parker would go back to practice blocking more. The two-time All-American was a unanimous selection in 1956 when he also won the Outland Trophy.

4. No school has produced more Rimington Trophy winners than Ohio State and Alabama, both of whom have had three recipients of the award. LeCharles Bentley was the second-ever winner in 2001 when he was also a consensus All-American and the Big Ten Offensive Lineman of the Year. The Buckeyes are the only program to have winners in consecutive years: Pat Elflein won the award in 2016 followed by Billy Price in 2017. Elflein was a unanimous All-American in 2016 and was also named the Big Ten Offensive Lineman of the Year. Price was a first-team All-American guard in 2016 before moving to center and becoming a first-team All-American center and the Big Ten Offensive Lineman of the Year in 2017.

5. Bill Willis broke the color barrier at Ohio State and in professional football during his impressive career. He was the Buckeyes' first black All-American in 1943 and then repeated the feat in 1944 before becoming one of four players to integrate professional football when he joined his college coach, Paul Brown, with the Cleveland Browns of the All-American Football Conference. Willis faced plenty of racial injustice during his time at Ohio State, including not being able to live on campus, so he instead commuted from his home in East Columbus by bus or hitchhiking. He was also stranded in Philadelphia after running the Penn Relays with the Buckeyes because he couldn't stay with the team at the hotel.

6. Dan Wilkinson needed plenty of help to get him to Ohio State and playing football for the Buckeyes. Wilkinson was more than 300 pounds for most of high school and didn't seem to have much direction in life even on the football field. His family kept trying to talk to him about his potential, but it didn't really click with Wilkinson until Ohio State began recruiting him as a senior. Still, Wilkinson had poor test scores and had to work through the summer until he qualified academically and joined the Buckeyes just a month before the start of the 1991 season. He redshirted as a freshman because he was 60 pounds overweight and that seemed to kickstart him onto his successful career. He was an All-Big Ten honoree in both 1992 and 1993 and was an All-American in 1993, leading him to be the 1st overall pick in the 1994 NFL Draft.

7. Thomas Johnson earned the nickname Pepper from his aunt, who was amused by the fact the young boy would sprinkle black pepper on his corn flakes in the morning. He brought plenty of spice to the Ohio State defense as well, earning All-American status as a senior in 1985. Johnson turned a lot of heads when he committed to Ohio State despite playing his high school football in Michigan, but he turned into one of the greatest defensive players in Buckeyes history with 379 total tackles.

8. Chris Spielman was famous around the country before he even set foot on campus at Ohio State. He was the first high school student ever to appear on a Wheaties box, and he introduced himself to the Ohio State faithful in notable fashion in his first game. Despite Oregon State moving the ball well to open the 1984 season, defensive coordinator Bob Tucker hadn't put Spielman in the game. Spielman spent the first half trying to plead with his coaches to play him, and Ohio State coach Earle Bruce asked Tucker at halftime why Spielman wasn't playing. When Tucker replied that Spielman was just a freshman and wasn't ready, Bruce told Tucker to put Spielman in. In the second half, Spielman racked up 10 tackles, deflected a pass, and forced the fumble that sealed the Buckeyes' victory over the Beavers.

9. A.J. Hawk's Ohio State teammates might have been more upset with the lack of respect Hawk received from the national awards circuit in 2005 than Hawk himself. In 2005, Hawk was a unanimous All-American selection as

well as the Big Ten's Defensive Player of the Year and the Lombardi Award winner. However, he was a finalist for the Lott Trophy as the nation's most impactful player on defense, the Butkus Award as the best linebacker in the country, and the Bednarik Award for the best defensive player in the county, but he didn't win any of those. The latter two awards went to Penn State linebacker Paul Posluszny, who was a consensus All-American but was beaten out by Hawk for his own conference's honor. It led Ohio State teammate Bobby Carpenter to tell ESPN, "I'm not too sure how you can be Big Ten [Defensive] Player of the Year, a unanimous first-team All-American, and not win the Butkus or Lott or Bednarik."

10. Mike Vrabel's final two years in Columbus rewrote the Ohio State record books in tremendous fashion. He was a first-team All-American in 1995 and 1996 and set the single-season record for sacks and tackles for loss in 1994 and 1995. However, as good as he was on the field, Vrabel admitted to struggling when he first got into coaching. After coming on in 2011 to coach linebackers under former teammate Luke Fickell, Vrabel had a chance to interview to keep his job at Ohio State under Urban Meyer. His first interview was horrific, but Meyer called him that night and offered him a redo the following day. Vrabel aced that interview and was hired to the staff at Ohio State before eventually becoming an NFL head coach in 2018 with the Tennessee Titans.

CHAPTER 7:

NO AIR ZONE

QUIZ TIME!

1. Ohio State has never allowed more than 4,000 yards passing in a season.

    a. True
    b. False

2. Who holds the Ohio State record for most interceptions in a career?

    a. Shawn Springs
    b. Bradley Roby
    c. Mike Sensibaugh
    d. Craig Cassady

3. Who is the only Buckeyes defensive back to return three interceptions for touchdowns in his career?

    a. Neal Colzie
    b. Malcolm Jenkins
    c. Malik Hooker
    d. Bradley Roby

4. Who is NOT one of the three Buckeyes to return an interception 100 yards for a touchdown?

    a. Marlon Kerner
    b. Kurt Coleman
    c. Will Allen
    d. David Brown

5. Who sits atop the Ohio State record book for career pass breakups?

    a. Bradley Roby
    b. Ahmed Plummer
    c. Antoine Winfield
    d. Shawn Springs

6. Which Ohio State defensive back is one of two Buckeyes defenders to be a three-time first-team All-American alongside linebacker James Laurinaitis?

    a. Mike Sensibaugh
    b. Malcolm Jenkins
    c. Malik Hooker
    d. Mike Doss

7. Who was Ohio State's second winner of the Jim Thorpe Award?

    a. Antoine Winfield
    b. Shawn Springs
    c. Mike Doss
    d. Malcolm Jenkins

8. Which Ohio State defensive back is one of the namesakes for the Big Ten's award for the best defensive back of the season?

   a. Shawn Springs
   b. Mike Doss
   c. Dick LeBeau
   d. Jack Tatum

9. Which Ohio State defensive back is the only player in school history to return two punts for a touchdown in the same game?

   a. Garcia Lane
   b. Nate Clements
   c. Neal Colzie
   d. Mike Guess

10. Shawn Springs was the first defensive back to be named the Big Ten Defensive Player of the Year.

    a. True
    b. False

11. Who was Ohio State's first first-team All-American as a defensive back?

    a. Jack Tatum
    b. Ted Provost
    c. Arnie Chonko
    d. Mike Sensibaugh

12. Dick LeBeau's legal first name is Charles, and his middle name is Richard.

a. True

b. False

13. In which season was Jack Tatum named the national defensive player of the year and unanimous All-American?

    a. 1971
    b. 1970
    c. 1969
    d. 1968

14. Before Shawn Springs being named a first-team All-American in 1996, it was nearly 20 years between Buckeyes defensive backs earning the honor. Who was that last defensive back before Springs to be a first-team All-American?

    a. Tim Fox
    b. Vince Skillings
    c. Neal Colzie
    d. Ray Griffin

15. How many interceptions did Shawn Springs have in 1996 when he was a consensus All-American and the Big Ten Defensive Player of the Year?

    a. 5
    b. 3
    c. 1
    d. 0

16. Antoine Winfield led the nation in interceptions in 1998 when he won the Thorpe Award.

a. True

b. False

17. How many tackles did Mike Doss have in his career to lead all Ohio State defensive backs in the category?

    a. 319

    b. 331

    c. 346

    d. 362

18. What is NOT true of Malcolm Jenkins's four-year career at Ohio State?

    a. Four-year starter

    b. Won four Big Ten championships

    c. Undefeated against Michigan

    d. Played in two national championship games

19. Whose record did Bradley Roby tie in 2012 with 17 pass breakups in a single season?

    a. Ashton Youboty

    b. Chris Gamble

    c. Ahmed Plummer

    d. Shawn Springs

20. How many times has Ohio State returned an interception for a touchdown?

    a. 78

    b. 82

    c. 87

    d. 90

QUIZ ANSWERS

1. A – True

2. C – Mike Sensibaugh

3. C – Malik Hooker

4. B – Kurt Coleman

5. A – Bradley Roby

6. D – Mike Doss

7. D – Malcolm Jenkins

8. D – Jack Tatum

9. A – Garcia Lane

10. B – False

11. C – Arnie Chonko

12. A – True

13. B – 1970

14. D – Ray Griffin

15. D – 0

16. B – False

17. B – 331

18. A – Four-year starter

19. C – Ahmed Plummer

20. C – 87

DID YOU KNOW?

1. Dick LeBeau was the quarterback on the Ohio State freshman team in 1955 when Howard Cassady was winning the Heisman Trophy as a senior. Although they didn't speak to each other often, Cassady pulled LeBeau aside once the season was over and told him that he wanted LeBeau to use Cassady's locker the next season when LeBeau would be a halfback on the varsity roster. Cassady wrote a note to LeBeau that he left in the locker that talked about perseverance and the "Buckeye spirit," which LeBeau said was very meaningful to him.

2. Jack Tatum arrived in Columbus as a running back and that was how Woody Hayes planned when he recruited Tatum to Ohio State. Once on campus, however, Lou Holtz persuaded Hayes to play Tatum at defensive back, and he evolved into a fearsome tackler for the Buckeyes. Ohio State used Tatum in a variety of different ways, from covering the other team's top receiver to playing linebacker when needed. He ended up being a three-time first-team All-Big Ten defensive back in his three seasons on the varsity squad and was an All-American in 1969 and 1970. Tatum was the national defensive player of the year in 1970 and is now the namesake of the Big Ten's defensive back of the year award along with Michigan's Charles Woodson.

3. Mike Sensibaugh was overshadowed by Tatum's success, but Sensibaugh's name remains at the top of the record books. In 1969, Sensibaugh set the Ohio State record with nine interceptions and followed that with eight the following season, making him the only OSU player to have eight or more interceptions in a season twice. Sensibaugh also still holds the career record with 22 picks; his 17 in his final two years would be tied for the career record.

4. Shawn Springs is the son of former Buckeyes running back Ron Springs, so an official visit to Michigan seemed out of the question, let alone the cornerback committing to the Wolverines. Yet Michigan was the favorite for the younger Springs's services until a few days before signing day when he canceled his visit to Michigan and committed to the Buckeyes a few days later. He made a large impact in Columbus over three years, notably in 1996 when he was a consensus All-American despite not intercepting a pass and having just 39 tackles. It was his 15 pass breakups when teams dared to throw to his side of the field that seemingly convinced voters he was one of the best defensive backs in the nation despite him being shut out of the major national awards.

5. Antoine Winfield broke a lot of boundaries for Ohio State defensive backs, especially in 1997 and 1998 when he burst onto the scene. In 1997, he became the first cornerback to lead the team in tackles when he had 100 stops, 82 of which were unassisted. The following year,

Winfield became the first Ohio State player to win the Thorpe Award as the nation's best defensive back; although, like Springs, he had no interceptions in 1998 when he was also a consensus All-American. He ended his career with 224 solo tackles, the first non-linebacker to reach that milestone for the Buckeyes.

6. Ahmed Plummer was the star of Ohio State's 6-6 season in 1999 and was voted the team's MVP as well as the defensive player of the year and defensive back of the year. A year after setting the Ohio State record with 17 pass breakups in 1998, Plummer was the Buckeyes' only first-team All-Big Ten selection in 1999 and was also a semifinalist for the Thorpe Award. He left the school as the program's leader, with 34 career breakups.

7. Mike Doss had no idea what he would do after the 2001 season. He had the chance to return to school for his senior year, but he could have made himself eligible for the NFL Draft. He was already a two-time first-team All-American safety, and he was highly rated by NFL scouts. But, when he walked into the room to announce his decision in January of 2002, he didn't know what he was going to tell the assembled media. What unfolded was a heartfelt speech that took many turns before he decided to stay at Ohio State. He had spent the hour before the press conference in his car speaking with his mother and praying about the decision. He went on to become Ohio State's seventh three-time first-team All-American, and he

helped the Buckeyes win a national championship in 2002.

8. Malcolm Jenkins made a name for himself on the field for Ohio State as the 2008 Thorpe Award winner, but, off the field, he had as big an impact on the campus and community. While at Ohio State, Jenkins pledged the majority black Omega Psi Phi fraternity, devoting much of his non-football and academic time to the organization. He served as the fraternity's vice president and stepmaster in 2008, helping to lead his brothers in step—an acrobatic rhythmic dance—to the national show in Alabama earlier that year. Through the organization, Jenkins also had a chance to mentor at-risk youth in Columbus who come to Ohio State's campus to study for the ACT, and the fraternity also uses step to reach kids in other parts of Columbus. When asked about his involvement in the fraternity, Jenkins told reporters, "That's why it's important to me, not necessarily my frat, but what my frat does. The relationships I have with these kids are something I really cherish."

9. Malik Hooker almost left Ohio State several times when he was redshirting as a true freshman in 2014. He would call his mother each time the thought crept into his brain, and his mother would shut him down each time. In the off-season between his redshirt season and his redshirt freshman year, he went for walks on weekends at his home in Pennsylvania, three hours east of Columbus, as he contemplated the decision. Hooker played mostly on

special teams in 2015, and the calls home to discuss transferring picked up again. This time, though, Hooker started to find his place in the spring practice of his second year at the school, and his natural ability took over. He was a unanimous first-team All-American in 2016 after intercepting seven passes and returning three for touchdowns as a redshirt sophomore.

10. Bradley Roby was originally committed to play wide receiver at Vanderbilt before ending up at Ohio State on the other side of the ball. His issue with the Commodores was simple: They just didn't win enough for him. The Buckeyes went 30-9 in his three seasons in Columbus, including a 12-0 season in 2012 when Ohio State was ineligible for the postseason. Roby intercepted eight passes and scored two touchdowns in his Ohio State career and left the school as its all-time leader in career pass breakups with 36 after tying Plummer's single-season record in 2012 with 17 breakups.

CHAPTER 8:

COACHING CAROUSEL

QUIZ TIME!

1. Who was the first coach in Ohio State's history?

   a. Jack Ryder

   b. John Eckstrom

   c. Alexander Lilley

   d. E.R. Sweetland

2. Which legendary coach led the Buckeyes to their first national championship?

   a. Wes Fesler

   b. Woody Hayes

   c. Paul Brown

   d. John Wilce

3. Including Woody Hayes, how many coaches have the Buckeyes had since hiring Hayes in 1951?

   a. 4

   b. 5

   c. 6

   d. 7

4. Every Ohio State non-interim coach from 1947 through the present has won a Big Ten championship.

    a. True
    b. False

5. Who was the first Ohio State coach to lead the Buckeyes to an undefeated, untied season?

    a. Carroll Widdoes
    b. John Eckstrom
    c. John Wilce
    d. Woody Hayes

6. What was Woody Hayes's first name?

    a. Wilson
    b. Wayne
    c. Woodrow
    d. Woodward

7. Which future Big Ten coach did NOT spend at least one season as an assistant at Ohio State?

    a. Darrell Hazel
    b. Mark Dantonio
    c. Tom Allen
    d. Tim Beckman

8. Which current NFL head coach spent one season as an assistant coach at Ohio State?

    a. Andy Reid
    b. John Harbaugh
    c. Matt Rhule
    d. Pete Carroll

9. Who was the last Ohio State coach to lead the Buckeyes to a losing record in the regular season?

    a. Jim Tressel

    b. Woody Hayes

    c. Luke Fickell

    d. John Cooper

10. Ohio State has never had an alumnus as its head coach.

    a. True

    b. False

11. How many Big Ten championships did Woody Hayes win as the Buckeyes' head coach?

    a. 13

    b. 15

    c. 11

    d. 17

12. Against whom was Woody Hayes's last game as Ohio State head coach?

    a. Clemson

    b. Baylor

    c. Michigan

    d. Southern California

13. In which year did Woody Hayes NOT win the Eddie Robinson Award as the national coach of the year?

    a. 1957

    b. 1968

    c. 1970

    d. 1975

14. John Cooper won 100 games as Ohio State's head coach.

    a. True

    b. False

15. John Cooper became infamous for his struggles against Michigan. How many times did Cooper's Buckeyes defeat the Wolverines during his tenure?

    a. 5

    b. 4

    c. 3

    d. 2

16. From which Ohio college did Ohio State hire Jim Tressel to replace John Cooper?

    a. Youngstown State

    b. Akron

    c. Mount Union

    d. Cincinnati

17. Which team did Jim Tressel never face in a national championship game?

    a. LSU

    b. Florida

    c. Miami

    d. Southern California

18. Urban Meyer and Jim Tressel combined to coach more All-Americans at Ohio State than Woody Hayes.

    a. True

    b. False

19. How many straight games did Urban Meyer win at the start of his career at Ohio State?

    a. 20
    b. 22
    c. 24
    d. 27

20. Who was the last Ohio State coach before Ryan Day in 2019 to be named the Big Ten Coach of the Year?

    a. Jim Tressel
    b. John Cooper
    c. Earle Bruce
    d. Woody Hayes

QUIZ ANSWERS

1. C – Alexander Lilley

2. C – Paul Brown

3. D – 7

4. A – True

5. C – John Wilce

6. B – Wayne

7. C – Tom Allen

8. D – Pete Carroll

9. D – John Cooper

10. B – False

11. A – 13

12. A – Clemson

13. C – 1970

14. A – True

15. D – 2

16. A – Youngstown State

17. D – Southern California

18. B – False

19. C – 24

20. C – Earle Bruce

DID YOU KNOW?

1. The Buckeyes have had many notable assistant coaches who went on to great acclaim at other schools. The most famous of them, of course, is Bo Schembechler, who was an assistant coach at Ohio State from 1958 to 1962 before leaving to become the head coach at Miami (Ohio) and then at rival Michigan. Lou Holtz was the cornerbacks coach at Ohio State in 1968, and he went on to lead Notre Dame to a national championship. Pete Carroll was also a one-year assistant in Columbus; he went on to win a national title at Southern California and a Super Bowl with the Seattle Seahawks. Larry Coker coached at Ohio State in 1993 and 1994 before winning a national title with Miami in 2001 and losing to the Buckeyes in the national championship game the following year. Nick Saban, who defeated Ohio State in the 2020 national title game for his seventh title, was an assistant at Ohio State in 1980-81.

2. Ohio State had a few interesting coaches in the first two decades of the program. The first coach of the Buckeyes, Alexander Lilley, was famous for riding his horses to practice each day. He was replaced by Jack Ryder, who was just 21 years old when he took the helm in Columbus in 1892. Charles Hickey was the coach who introduced the concession stand to Ohio State fans. Those first stands sold candy, popcorn, peanuts, and chrysanthemums to hungry Buckeyes fans.

3. John Wilce was Ohio State's first consistent head coach, holding the position from 1913 to 1928 and winning three Big Ten championships along the way. He was the coach when the Buckeyes joined the conference in 1913, and he led Ohio State to the first Rose Bowl in team history after the 1920 season. Wilce earned his medical degree from Ohio State in 1919 while coaching the team, and he resigned in 1928 to go into private practice. Six years later, in 1934, Wilce became the director of Ohio State's student health services after doing postgraduate research at Harvard and Columbia.

4. Paul Brown was a dominant high school coach in Ohio before the Buckeyes scooped him up to coach their team in 1941. He went 18-8-1 in three seasons in Columbus before he was drafted into the Navy as a lieutenant junior grade, and he left to report to the Great Lakes Naval Training Station, where he coached the football team. Throughout his tenure in the Navy, he was still technically Ohio State's coach, but he officially left that position after the war when he was given the chance to coach the professional football team in Cleveland that ended up being named after him.

5. Wes Fesler was a three-time All-American at Ohio State from 1928 through 1930 as an end for the Buckeyes. He was named the player of the year in the Big Ten as a senior in 1930, and he made contributions in three different sports at Ohio State. In addition to playing three years on the gridiron, Fesler also played basketball and

baseball for the Buckeyes for three seasons. Fesler was an assistant at Ohio State for one season, and then became the head coach at three different schools before returning to Columbus to coach the Buckeyes in 1947. Over four years as the Ohio State head coach, Fesler won 21 games, including the 1949 Big Ten championship and 1950 Rose Bowl.

6. The numbers from Woody Hayes's tenure at Ohio State are staggering and seem almost impossible for any coach to match in Columbus. Hayes won 13 Big Ten championships and five national titles and was named the national coach of the year three times during his Hall of Fame career at Ohio State. He coached 56 first-team All-Americans and won 205 games while leading the Buckeyes from 1951 through 1978. He was known for his love of military history, and he often quoted General George Patton to his players. He was a close personal friend of former president Richard Nixon. The former president delivered a eulogy at Hayes's funeral and told the story about their first meeting and how they spent the encounter discussing foreign policy per Hayes's request rather than football as Nixon was hoping.

7. Earle Bruce was responsible for molding many of the coaches who are currently making a tremendous impact on college football. Urban Meyer, who has won three national championships, including one at Ohio State, was a graduate assistant under Bruce, as was Michigan State head coach Mark Dantonio. Bruce came to Ohio State in

86

hopes of playing for the Buckeyes, but a knee injury ended his playing career and turned him onto coaching. Even though he coached at other places before and after his stint in Columbus, Ohio State always had a pull on his heart, and he spent 23 years as a radio analyst on the Ohio State broadcast after retiring from coaching.

8. Many criticized John Cooper for his results against Michigan, but the Buckeyes were extremely successful under Cooper. Ohio State finished in the top 10 nationally five times during his tenure, including number two finishes in 1996 and 1998. Cooper is the only coach to win the Rose Bowl as the coach of a Big Ten and a Pac-12 school, but his 111 wins over 13 seasons as Ohio State head coach was not enough to overcome his 2-10-1 record against Michigan.

9. Jim Tressel's exit from Ohio State was extremely ugly after the details of his ignorance were unraveled following the 2010 season. The coach played five players—including star quarterback Terrelle Pryor—during the season despite knowing that they had an arrangement with a local tattoo shop that violated NCAA rules. The players were suspended before the Sugar Bowl that season and for the first few games of the following year, and Tressel also was banned for his role. However, as more details emerged about Tressel's lies, he was eventually forced to resign from the post in May 2011. Tressel has recouped his image somewhat since taking over as the president of Youngstown State in 2014.

Though some students and alumni were hesitant about the move just three years removed from the fallout at Ohio State, Tressel has helped raise the academic profile of the school since being named the school's president.

10. Six months after Tressel's resignation, Ohio State hired Urban Meyer, who went on to win all 12 games in his first season as the Buckeyes dealt with the punishment for the violations committed under Tressel. Meyer won at least a share of the division title all seven years as Ohio State's coach, and he won the conference three times, including in 2014 when he led the Buckeyes to a national championship. His .901 winning percentage is the best among Ohio State coaches with at least three full seasons at the helm of the program.

CHAPTER 9:

CHAMPIONSHIP CALIBER

QUIZ TIME!

1. In which of these seasons did Ohio State go undefeated and untied without winning the national championship?

   a. 1944

   b. 1960

   c. 1975

   d. 1993

2. Who was the only school to beat Ohio State in 1942 when the program won its first national championship?

   a. Northwestern

   b. Michigan

   c. Wisconsin

   d. Pittsburgh

3. Who is the only member of the 1942 championship team to be enshrined in both the College Football and Pro Football Halls of Fame?

   a. Bill Willis

   b. Paul Brown

    c. Les Horvath

    d. Dante Lavelli

4. Who did Ohio State beat in the Rose Bowl to finish off its 1954 championship season?

    a. UCLA

    b. California

    c. Stanford

    d. Southern California

5. How many games did Ohio State play as the number one team in the country during the 1954 season?

    a. 5

    b. 4

    c. 3

    d. 2

6. Which team upset Ohio State at the Horseshoe to begin the 1957 season and then tied the Buckeyes at the start of the 1961 title-winning season?

    a. Washington

    b. Oklahoma

    c. SMU

    d. TCU

7. Ohio State split the national championship with Auburn in 1957.

    a. True

    b. False

8. Which team was ranked ahead of Ohio State in both the Associated Press and United Press International polls in 1961?

    a. Texas
    b. LSU
    c. Alabama
    d. Arkansas

9. Which organization ranked Ohio State as its national champion, allowing the Buckeyes to claim the 1961 title?

    a. American Football Coaches Association
    b. Football Writers Association of America
    c. *USA Today*
    d. National Football Foundation

10. The 1968 national champions were the first to win the title while going undefeated and untied.

    a. True
    b. False

11. What was Southern California ranked by the United Press International entering the 1969 Rose Bowl against the Buckeyes to close out the 1968 season?

    a. 4th
    b. 3rd
    c. 2nd
    d. 1st

12. Which team tripped up the Buckeyes in the 1971 Rose Bowl to ruin Ohio State's run at a perfect season?

a. California

b. Stanford

c. Oregon

d. Washington

13. In addition to Jim Stillwagon, who was the other unanimous first-team All-American on the 1970 championship squad?

a. Jack Tatum

b. Tim Anderson

c. John Brockington

d. John DeLeone

14. Who scored the winning touchdown for Ohio State in the second overtime of the 2003 Fiesta Bowl against Miami?

a. Chris Gamble

b. Craig Krenzel

c. Maurice Clarett

d. Michael Jenkins

15. The 2002 national championship squad was the first to NOT end its season in the Rose Bowl.

a. True

b. False

16. Who returned the opening kickoff for a touchdown in the loss to Florida in the 2006 National Championship Game?

a. Andre Amos

b. Ted Ginn Jr.

c. Ray Small

d. Antonio Pittman

17. How many consecutive points did LSU score to overcome an early 10-0 deficit against Ohio State in the 2007 National Championship Game?

    a. 17
    b. 24
    c. 28
    d. 31

18. Where was the 2014 College Football Playoff National Championship Game played?

    a. Pasadena, California
    b. New Orleans
    c. Atlanta
    d. Arlington, Texas

19. Ohio State defeated Oregon to win the first national championship to be decided by the College Football Playoff.

    a. True
    b. False

20. Who rushed for two touchdowns to lead the offense in Ohio State's loss to Alabama in the 2020 College Football Playoff National Championship Game?

    a. Chris Olave
    b. Trey Sermon
    c. Justin Fields
    d. Master Teague III

QUIZ ANSWERS

1. A – 1944

2. C – Wisconsin

3. A – Bill Willis

4. D – Southern California

5. C – 3

6. D – TCU

7. A – True

8. C – Alabama

9. B – Football Writers Association of America

10. B – False

11. C – 2nd

12. B – Stanford

13. A – Jack Tatum

14. C – Maurice Clarett

15. B – False

16. B – Ted Ginn Jr.

17. D – 31

18. D – Arlington, Texas

19. A – True

20. D – Master Teague III

DID YOU KNOW?

1. The only loss in Ohio State's 1942 national championship season was a 17-7 defeat by Wisconsin that came with a caveat. The Buckeyes were down a few key players and coaches who fell ill during the trip to Madison. The culprit was a water fountain at the train station in Chicago before Ohio State boarded its train for Madison. The debilitating virus crippled roughly half of the Buckeyes team for the game, ruining Ohio State's chance at perfection.

2. The 1954 team was denied a chance at playing UCLA, the team that would tie the Buckeyes for the national championship that season, because of the Rose Bowl's rule that teams could not play in the bowl game in consecutive seasons. Instead, the Buckeyes handled Southern California in the 1955 Rose Bowl to secure a third perfect season. Though it wasn't until the following year that Howard Cassady would win the Heisman Trophy, he came up with a pair of huge plays defensively during the regular season to spur the Buckeyes to an unbeaten record. Cassady intercepted a pass against California that led to Ohio State sealing its win over the Golden Bears with a touchdown, and he flipped the momentum of a battle against number two Wisconsin with an 88-yard pick-six that gave Ohio State the lead.

3. After losing to TCU in the 1957 opener, Ohio State seemed to be in some trouble at Washington in the second game

95

of the season. But one play from Don Sutherin changed the entire course of the season for the Buckeyes. Sutherin's 81-yard punt return touchdown broke a 7-7 deadlock, and Ohio State pulled away with the momentum after that play. Sutherin added to his legacy by booting the game-winning field goal in the Rose Bowl that season, but, even years later, Woody Hayes pointed to the punt return as the reason the Buckeyes were named the United Press International champion in 1957. "Sutherin's punt return was the play that turned our '57 season around. We just seemed to gel from that point forward."

4. The 1961 Ohio State Buckeyes were forced to end their season against Michigan after a controversial vote of the faculty to decline the Rose Bowl's invitation. The Buckeyes had won eight straight games after tying TCU to open the season, but there were tensions behind the scenes with the faculty's animosity toward the football team. The faculty council rejected the bid 28-25 in a heated vote, denying the Buckeyes a chance to face UCLA in the Rose Bowl. Among the biggest objections to the game were the disruption to the football players' academic schedules and the damage to the school's academic reputation because Ohio State was becoming known for its football team.

5. The "Super Sophomores" of the 1968 national championship team were the first to push Woody Hayes out of his comfort zone on offense. With Rex Kern at the helm as the quarterback, offensive coordinator George Chaump persuaded Hayes to use the I-formation, which

allowed the Buckeyes to spread the field better with their rushing attack. The 1968 squad averaged 84 plays per game with a hurry-up tempo that would fit in with the modern game. The regular-season finale was a blowout for Ohio State, which rolled to a 50-14 victory over Michigan, and it was the game that brought the world the classic Woody Hayes quote about going for two at the end of the game. When asked about the decision, Hayes just quipped, "Because I couldn't go for three." The little-known story is that Ohio State also didn't have a long snapper ready for the extra point after the final touchdown, so the players also had a role in why the Buckeyes went for two points.

6. The 1970 title is the most contested of the eight national championships that Ohio State claims to have won. The 1961 team went undefeated, though it had one tie, and it was denied the chance to play a postseason game. So claiming a pre-bowl national championship isn't the worst offense, but, in 1970, the National Football Federation handed out its national championship distinction before the bowl games and awarded the honor to the Buckeyes. Of course, the Buckeyes would then lose in the Rose Bowl, ruining their chance at perfection and slipping in the final polls. So while the school claims eight national titles, many would argue Ohio State only has six because two of them were not awarded in the polls or title games.

7. In 2018, ESPN ranked the 21 national champions of the BCS era, and the 2002 Buckeyes were ranked dead last. The major knock against the Buckeyes was the close games it played in down the final stretch of the season and the fact they weren't dominant. This is despite the fact the Buckeyes were the first team to win 14 games in a season and just one of nine teams on the list to complete the season unbeaten. Since 1998, when the BCS was implemented, only 12 teams have managed to go unbeaten and win the national title, and 11 have lost at least one game along the road to the championship. The title was also the first unanimous national championship for the Big Ten since the Buckeyes steamrolled the competition in 1968.

8. The 2002 Buckeyes were the first number two team to beat the number one team in the BCS era, and the 2014 Buckeyes were the first to win the College Football Playoff. There was a lot of controversy over Ohio State's inclusion as the number four team in the inaugural playoff over Big 12 co-champion Baylor, who beat fellow co-champion TCU and had lost just once that season like the Buckeyes. Yet the committee gave Ohio State the nod, and the Buckeyes shocked many by upsetting Alabama in the Sugar Bowl behind 230 yards on the ground from Ezekiel Elliott, a Sugar Bowl record. Elliott rushed for 246 yards in the national championship game against Oregon and finished the two-game playoff run with six rushing touchdowns combined.

9. Ohio State and Oklahoma are the only teams to play in and lose consecutive national championship games. The Buckeyes' losses came in the 2007 and 2008 title games. Ohio State scored first in both contests, returning the opening kickoff for a touchdown against Florida in 2007 and scoring the first 10 points in 2008 against LSU, but they could not sustain the momentum to seal another national championship.

10. The 1944 Ohio State Buckeyes could claim a "civilian national championship" because they finished number two in the country behind Army despite winning all nine of their games. It was Carroll Widdoes's first season in charge as the "acting" head coach with Paul Brown on assignment with the Navy, and it was Ohio State's first unbeaten, untied season since 1916, before a national championship even being awarded. The only other Ohio State team to go unbeaten without being named the national champion was the 2012 squad, which was ineligible for the postseason due to NCAA violations.

CHAPTER 10:

GOING BOWLING

QUIZ TIME!

1. Ohio State won its first appearance in the Rose Bowl.

   a. True

   b. False

2. What was the first bowl game Ohio State played besides the Rose Bowl?

   a. Sugar

   b. Orange

   c. Gator

   d. Peach

3. Which team has Ohio State never played in the Rose Bowl?

   a. Arizona State

   b. Washington

   c. Washington State

   d. UCLA

4. How many times has Ohio State appeared in the Rose Bowl?

    a. 14

    b. 15

    c. 17

    d. 18

5. Who kicked the winning field goal to give Ohio State its first bowl win in the 1950 Rose Bowl?

    a. Tad Weed

    b. John Stungis

    c. Vic Janowicz

    d. Jimmy Hague

6. The 1969 Rose Bowl was the first to feature two unbeaten teams since the game began taking the Big Ten and Pac-8 champions.

    a. True

    b. False

7. Ohio State went to four consecutive Rose Bowls from 1973 through 1976 but went 1-3 in those games. Which Rose Bowl did the Buckeyes win?

    a. 1973

    b. 1974

    c. 1975

    d. 1976

8. The 1978 Gator Bowl was famous for Woody Hayes punching which Clemson player?

a. Jim Stuckey

b. Steve Fuller

c. Charlie Bauman

d. Jerry Butler

9. Who did Ohio State beat in the 1981 Liberty Bowl to snap a four-game losing streak in postseason contests?

a. Navy

b. Air Force

c. Army

d. BYU

10. Whose pick-six on the second play of the second half in the 1985 Citrus Bowl was the deciding score in Ohio State's win over BYU?

a. Larry Kolic

b. Michael Kee

c. William White

d. Terry White

11. How many interceptions did Ohio State have in the 1987 Cotton Bowl against Texas A&M to set the school record for interceptions in a bowl game?

a. 8

b. 7

c. 6

d. 5

12. Who came off the bench to throw two touchdown passes and earn Most Valuable Player honors while leading Ohio State to a win in the 1997 Rose Bowl?

    a. Pepe Pearson
    b. Stanley Jackson
    c. Joe Germaine
    d. Bobby Hoying

13. Which team defeated Ohio State in back-to-back appearances in the Outback Bowl in 2001 and 2002?

    a. Tennessee
    b. Florida
    c. Kentucky
    d. South Carolina

14. The first time Ohio State and Southern California faced off in a bowl game that wasn't the Rose Bowl was in 2017 when they played in which New Year's Six Bowl Game?

    a. Cotton Bowl
    b. Fiesta Bowl
    c. Orange Bowl
    d. Sugar Bowl

15. When was the last time Ohio State entered a bowl game NOT ranked in the top 10?

    a. 2001 Outback Bowl
    b. 2004 Alamo Bowl
    c. 2009 Fiesta Bowl
    d. 2012 Gator Bowl

16. Ohio State has pitched a shutout in a bowl game.

    a. True
    b. False

17. Who holds the Buckeyes' record for most rushing yards in a bowl game?

    a. Keith Byars
    b. Raymont Harris
    c. Carlos Hyde
    d. Ezekiel Elliott

18. The same player holds the Ohio State record for most receiving yards and most receptions in a bowl game.

    a. True
    b. False

19. Which team did Ohio State beat for the first time in program history in the 2021 Sugar Bowl?

    a. Georgia
    b. Alabama
    c. Clemson
    d. Auburn

20. Which Ohio State bowl record did the Buckeyes NOT set in that 2021 Sugar Bowl victory?

    a. Points
    b. Touchdowns
    c. First downs
    d. Total yards

QUIZ ANSWERS

1. B – False

2. B – Orange

3. C – Washington State

4. A – 14

5. D – Jimmy Hague

6. A – True

7. B – 1974

8. C – Charlie Bauman

9. A – Navy

10. A – Larry Kolic

11. D – 5

12. C – Joe Germaine

13. D – South Carolina

14. A – Cotton Bowl

15. D – 2012 Gator Bowl

16. B – False

17. D – Ezekiel Elliott

18. B – False

19. C – Clemson

20. C – First downs

DID YOU KNOW?

1. The Buckeyes picked up their first bowl victory on New Year's Day 1950 when they avenged their loss in the only other bowl game in program history with a win over California in the Rose Bowl. The game was tied late in the fourth quarter when California was forced to punt from deep in its own end. The snap was low, and the Golden Bears' punter was forced to use his weaker foot, dribbling it out of bounds at California's 13-yard line. The Buckeyes were facing fourth-and-two, and coach Wes Fesler sent out backup quarterback Dick Widdoes to hold for Jimmy Hague's field goal attempt. The players, though, wanted to try for the touchdown and sent Widdoes back to the sideline. By the time the power struggle ended, the Buckeyes had been penalized for delay of game, and Hague then booted the winning field goal.

2. For three straight years, Ohio State faced off with Southern California in the Rose Bowl, and the 1975 edition was the closest of the trio. After the two teams split a pair of blowouts the previous two seasons, Ohio State entered the 1975 contest with ambitions of a national championship. Ohio State scored on its first two possessions of the fourth quarter to take a 17-10 lead, and the ensuing kickoff had the Trojans starting at their own 17-yard line. USC proceeded to march the 83 yards for a touchdown, the final 38 of which came on the touchdown

pass. But the Trojans then decided to go for two, which they converted for a slim one-point lead with two minutes left. Cornelius Greene led the Buckeyes back to midfield, but Tom Skladany's 62-yard attempt fell short of the uprights on the final play of the game.

3. In 1976, Ohio State returned to Pasadena as an undefeated team and faced UCLA for a chance at another national championship. The Buckeyes had soundly defeated the Bruins earlier in the season and were heavy favorites to close out the unbeaten season for a seventh national championship. However, Ohio State could not convert an overwhelming advantage in time of possession in the first half into more than a 3-0 lead. The field goal on the opening drive of the game was about as well as the Buckeyes would play on offense as UCLA came out and scored 16 points in the third quarter to take a large lead. Pete Johnson rushed for a touchdown early in the fourth quarter to cut the lead to one score, but many blamed Woody Hayes for overthinking himself several times in the game by abandoning the run and having Cornelius Greene pass the ball 18 times. Greene was intercepted twice, both in the fourth quarter, including once on a drive that began at the UCLA 35 after an Ohio State interception and personal foul penalty on the Bruins.

4. The Big Ten allowed a non-champion to play in a bowl game for the first time in 1975, and the Buckeyes had a chance to take advantage of the opportunity the following year after winning the conference and playing in the Rose

Bowl. Many of the players were hesitant about playing in the 1977 Orange Bowl after getting trounced by Michigan in the season finale, but Woody Hayes said Ohio State would face Colorado in Miami on New Year's Day 1977. The Buffalos scored the first 10 points of the game, but the contest turned when Hayes inserted Rod Gerard at quarterback. Gerard had missed the last four games of the season with a bone chip in his back, but he ran for 17 yards on his first snap and 81 yards total in the game as the Buckeyes revamped their offense. Jeff Logan lined up at fullback, and Rod Springs was at halfback in a new two-tailback set, and Ohio State ran 71 times for 271 yards to score 27 unanswered points in the win.

5. Clemson beat Ohio State, 17-15, in the 1978 Gator Bowl but nothing about what happened on the field became the story of this game. Woody Hayes had been known to lose his temper, so it wasn't a surprise that he lost it again when Art Schlichter was intercepted deep in Clemson territory on what turned out to be Ohio State's final drive of the night. The surprise was that Hayes grabbed Clemson defensive lineman Charlie Bauman's jersey and punched the player in the chest after Bauman intercepted the pass and was pushed out of bounds in front of Hayes. The Ohio State coach kept trying to go at Bauman while Bauman retreated, and Buckeyes captain Byron Cato ended up having to pull his own coach away from the scene. It would be the lasting image of Hayes's final game as Ohio State head coach as he was fired the next morning for throwing the punch.

6. Everyone expected the 1985 Citrus Bowl to be a showcase of the vast offensive talent on both sides, but instead, it was a defensive struggle that saw the Buckeyes fail to score an offensive touchdown. Fortunately, Ohio State intercepted BYU quarterback Robbie Bosco four times, all in the second half, and forced two fumbles to keep the Cougars at bay. Bosco did throw a 38-yard touchdown pass on a broken play to help BYU take a 7-3 lead into halftime, but Larry Kolic intercepted Bosco on the second play of the third quarter and rumbled 14 yards into the end zone for Ohio State's only touchdown. Kolic intercepted another pass later in the game and then William White and Terry White each intercepted Bosco passes into the end zone to seal the victory and stop BYU's dangerous drives from ending in points.

7. Ohio State entered the 1997 Rose Bowl with the bitter taste of disappointment that it would not be playing for a national championship. The Buckeyes were sluggish to start on offense, and John Cooper turned to Joe Germaine at quarterback to spark the team. Germaine delivered with a 72-yard pass to Demetrius Stanley that gave Ohio State a 14-10 lead, which the Buckeyes held into the fourth quarter. However, Arizona State blocked a field goal attempt, and the Sun Devils turned that into a Jake Plummer rushing touchdown to reclaim the lead. With 1:33 on the clock and 65 yards to go for the win, Germaine engineered the winning drive, finishing it with a five-yard toss to David Boston with 19 seconds left to secure the

victory. Germaine completed nine of his 17 attempts for 131 yards and the two scores while starter Stanley Jackson completed just six of 14 for 59 yards.

8. The Ohio State record books cannot claim that the Buckeyes won the 2011 Sugar Bowl but that doesn't mean the Buckeyes did not defeat Arkansas in the game. Terrell Pryor threw for 221 yards and two touchdowns and also ran for 115 yards on 15 carries to lead the Buckeyes to a 31-26 victory. It was Ohio State's first win over an SEC school in the postseason, an honor that now belongs to Ohio State's win over Alabama in the 2015 Sugar Bowl. The Buckeyes led 28-10 at halftime and extended the lead to 31-13 with four minutes left in the third quarter, but the Razorbacks clawed to within five points and had the ball late in the game. But Solomon Thomas intercepted Ryan Mallett with less than a minute left to seal the win for the Buckeyes, which would later be vacated due to NCAA violations.

9. Due to the Fiesta Bowl being a semifinal for the College Football Playoff after the 2016 season, there were two Fiesta Bowls in the 2016 calendar year, and Ohio State played in both of them. The Buckeyes defeated Notre Dame 44-28 on New Year's Day behind four touchdown runs from Ezekiel Elliott that day. Then the Buckeyes squared off against Clemson on New Year's Eve in the national semifinals and were thoroughly dismantled 31-0.

10. Ohio State got its revenge on Clemson in the 2021 Sugar Bowl, another national semifinal for the College Football

Playoff. The Buckeyes had lost to the Tigers in the semifinals of the 2016 and 2019 College Football Playoff and had lost to the Tigers twice in previous meetings in bowl games. But, on New Year's Day 2021, the Buckeyes scored four straight touchdowns in the first half to turn a 14-7 deficit into a 35-14 halftime lead. Justin Fields completed 22 of his 28 passes for 385 yards and six touchdowns, tying the school record for most touchdown passes in a game. Trey Sermon added 193 rushing yards and scored once, but the story was how well the Buckeyes' defense was able to contain Clemson's offense in the middle two quarters, limiting the Tigers to five punts and forcing fumbles on seven drives in the second and third quarters.

CHAPTER 11:

DRAFT DAY

QUIZ TIME!

1. Who was the first Ohio State player drafted into the NFL?

    a. Dick Heekin

    b. Merle Wendt

    c. Gomer Jones

    d. Sid Gillman

2. Who did the Philadelphia Eagles draft with the 2nd overall pick in 1938, becoming the first team to draft an Ohio State player in the 1st round?

    a. Don Scott

    b. Charley Hamrick

    c. Dick Nardi

    d. James McDonald

3. Who was the first 1st overall pick in Ohio State's history?

    a. Tom Cousineau

    b. Bob Ferguson

    c. Dan Wilkinson

    d. Orlando Pace

4. In which round did the Cleveland Rams select Les Horvath after his Heisman Trophy-winning season?

    a. 6th
    b. 5th
    c. 4th
    d. 7th

5. Which of these other Heisman Trophy winners from Ohio State was also NOT a 1st round pick in the NFL Draft?

    a. Eddie George
    b. Archie Griffin
    c. Howard Cassady
    d. Vic Janowicz

6. Paul Brown drafted Bill Willis to the Cleveland Browns in 1946.

    a. True
    b. False

7. Ohio State first had two 1st round picks in 1959 when Don Clark was picked 7th and which teammate was picked with the 8th selection?

    a. James Houston
    b. Dick LeBeau
    c. Frank Kremblas
    d. Dan James

8. The Cleveland Browns were the only NFL team to select an Ohio State player in the 1960 NFL Draft.

    a. True
    b. False

9. Paul Warfield was a 1st round draft pick of the Browns in 1964, but which AFL team used a 4th round pick on the receiver that same season?

   a. Oakland Raiders
   b. Buffalo Bills
   c. Kansas City Chiefs
   d. San Diego Chargers

10. Only two Buckeyes were ever drafted in the 1st round of the AFL Draft, Bob Ferguson in 1962 and which running back in 1964?

    a. Bo Scott
    b. Matt Snell
    c. Dave Francis
    d. Tom Barrington

11. Who was NOT one of the four 1st round picks Ohio State had in 1971?

    a. John Brockington
    b. Jack Tatum
    c. Jan White
    d. Tim Anderson

12. Defensive back Tim Fox was drafted before two-time Heisman Trophy winner Archie Griffin in 1976.

    a. True
    b. False

13. Which of these players was a 1st round pick in the 1980s?

    a. Chris Spielman
    b. Pepper Johnson

c. Art Schlichter

d. Cris Carter

14. Which of these Ohio State standouts was NOT a top-10 pick in the NFL Draft?

    a. Rickey Dudley

    b. Terry Glenn

    c. Eddie George

    d. Shawn Springs

15. Which team drafted Mike Vrabel in the 3rd round of the 1997 NFL Draft?

    a. Cincinnati Bengals

    b. New England Patriots

    c. Dallas Cowboys

    d. Pittsburgh Steelers

16. In which year did Ohio State have a school-record five players drafted in the 1st round for the first time?

    a. 1996

    b. 1999

    c. 2006

    d. 2016

17. Which of these pairs of Ohio State players were NOT selected with consecutive picks in the 1st round?

    a. Joey Bosa and Ezekiel Elliott

    b. A.J. Hawk and Donte Whitner

    c. Chase Young and Jeff Okudah

    d. Chris Gamble and Michael Jenkins

18. Which undrafted former Ohio State player has appeared in the most Pro Bowls?

    a. Dante Lavelli
    b. Jim Tyrer
    c. Ernie Wright
    d. Lou Groza

19. When was the last time Ohio State did NOT have a player drafted in the 1st round?

    a. 2015
    b. 2014
    c. 2013
    d. 2012

20. Ohio State has had a player drafted in all 32 spots of the modern-day 1st round except for the 17th overall pick.

    a. True
    b. False

QUIZ ANSWERS

1. C – Gomer Jones

2. D – James McDonald

3. A – Tom Cousineau

4. A – 6th

5. D – Vic Janowicz

6. B – False

7. D – Dan James

8. A – True

9. B – Buffalo Bills

10. B – Matt Snell

11. C – Jan White

12. A – True

13. C – Art Schlichter

14. C – Eddie George

15. D – Pittsburgh Steelers

16. C – 2006

17. B – A.J. Hawk and Donte Whitner

18. D – Lou Groza

19. A – 2015

20. A – True

DID YOU KNOW?

1. When the Cleveland Browns decided to draft Paul Warfield in 1964, they figured the Ohio State halfback would play defensive back in the NFL. That was the plan, at least, when they brought Warfield and the rest of their rookies to a one-day mini-camp after the draft. However, the Browns knew Warfield had also played a pseudo-receiver role with the Buckeyes, so they tested him with the receivers as well during the practice session. They made the decision that day to use Warfield at wide receiver and helped guide him through learning the position after having no experience as a receiver in his previous football career.

2. The first rookie ever to hold out for an entire season was former Ohio State kicker and punter Tom Skladany. He was the first specialist ever offered a scholarship to a Big Ten school, and he was a 2nd round pick of the Cleveland Browns in 1977. Skladany was represented by another Ohio State graduate, Howard Slusher, who Browns owner Art Modell once called the biggest thorn in the side of professional football. Skladany never signed with the Browns. The Rams backed out of a deal to trade for Skladany's rights for two 2nd round picks, and Cleveland eventually shipped the disgruntled punter to the Lions for 3rd and 7th round selections.

3. Two years later, Tom Cousineau was a higher-profile holdout after being selected as the 1ˢᵗ overall pick in the 1979 NFL Draft by the Buffalo Bills. Cousineau had wanted his agent to come with him to Buffalo to negotiate the contract after he was selected, but the Bills only paid for Cousineau to make the trip to Buffalo. Then the Bills sent in a low-ball offer of $1.2 million over five years, so Cousineau balked and signed an $850,000 deal for three years in the Canadian Football League with the Montreal Alouettes. He eventually returned to the NFL with the Browns after Cleveland traded for his rights, but Cousineau has since admitted he might have some regrets over how the situation played out.

4. Dan Wilkinson ended his third year at Ohio State as a likely top-five pick in the 1994 NFL Draft. His dominance in the trenches for the Buckeyes impressed NFL scouts enough that he was a consensus top-five selection. But then he got to the scouting combine. He bench-pressed 225 pounds an astounding 34 times, several more repetitions than any other defensive lineman. At his pro day, the 300-pound lineman clocked a 4.7-second 40-yard dash. He rocketed up draft boards to become the presumptive 1ˢᵗ overall pick, which was held by the Cincinnati Bengals. Then the questions started to circulate about whether or not the Bengals would be able to afford to pay Wilkinson or if they would have to trade the pick or his rights to someone else. The Arizona Cardinals and

New England Patriots made strong offers for the pick, but the Bengals held strong and drafted Wilkinson.

5. Terry Glenn caused a lot of trouble in New England through no fault of his own after the Patriots drafted the Ohio State receiver with the 7th overall pick in 1996. Bill Parcells was coaching the Patriots at the time and was upset with New England's front office for drafting another offensive weapon instead of the defensive player he preferred. He famously commented on the situation by telling reporters, "If they want you to cook the dinner, at least they ought to let you shop for some of the groceries." Glenn was the preferred choice of owner Bob Kraft and general manager Bobby Grier, and it turned out to be the correct choice as Glenn set a rookie record with 90 catches to help New England advance to the Super Bowl that season.

6. Dick Vermeil spent a lot of time around the Ohio State football program when he was working on the ABC college football broadcasts. His final game in the ABC booth was the Buckeyes' win over Arizona State in the 1997 Rose Bowl. The former NFL coach was lured back into the league after that game and took over the St. Louis Rams, who owned the number six pick in the draft. Vermeil might have jokingly said on air that offensive tackle Orlando Pace would be his first pick if he got back into the NFL, but, after being hired by the Rams, he tried to make it a reality. The coach won a dinner from Rams president John Shaw by trading the number six pick as

well as 3rd, 4th, and 7th round selections in the 1997 NFL Draft to the New York Jets for the 1st overall pick and the right to draft Pace.

7. After leading top-ranked Ohio State to a win over number two Michigan in 2006 and securing a berth in the national championship game, Troy Smith was destined to be a 1st round pick. He won the Heisman Trophy that season and looked dominant enough to justify being a high selection in the 2007 NFL Draft. But a poor performance in the national title game against Florida, a poor showing at the Senior Bowl a few weeks later, and some average performances at the combine and pro day left Smith plummeting down draft boards. As ESPN's Todd McShay put it to the *Columbus Dispatch* in the lead-up to the draft, "Everything since the end of the regular season, since that Michigan game, has been negative in regards to Troy Smith." Smith was frustrated when reporters would broach the subject, but the Ohio State legend still had to wait until the 5th round when the Ravens drafted him with the 174th overall pick.

8. In June 2011, Terrelle Pryor announced that he was going to enter the NFL's Supplemental Draft, forgoing his final season at Ohio State after a turbulent off-season that included Jim Tressel's resignation and an impending five-week suspension for accepting impermissible benefits. In a span of 96 hours in August, his whole world was put into overdrive for the draft process. On August 18, Pryor was told he would be eligible for the August 22 draft but

would be suspended for the first five weeks of the season and would not be allowed to practice with his team during that stretch. He held a workout on August 20 for 17 teams to show off his skills, and two days later, he was drafted in the 3rd round by the Oakland Raiders.

9. The Dallas Cowboys seemed pretty intent on drafting Ezekiel Elliott with the 4th overall pick in the 2016 NFL Draft. Immediately after the Rams selected Jared Goff with the first pick, Dallas called Elliott to make sure that no other team had reached out to him. Elliott wanted to go to Dallas, but he and his family were nervous when Dallas was on the clock and the cameras in the green room at the NFL Draft in Chicago started to circle Laremy Tunsil's table. The Elliotts assumed that the Cowboys had made a trade or were going to select Tunsil, and their sights briefly went to Chicago, who had hired Ohio State running backs coach Stan Drayton. However, Elliott's phone rang minutes later, and the Cowboys officially informed him that they had drafted the running back. "He just put his head in his hands," his mother, Dawn, told the *Dallas Morning News*, "and I knew he was crying, and that's when I knew."

10. Ohio State has had 84 players drafted in the 1st round of the NFL Draft, and 33 of them have been chosen since 2000. Exactly one-third of those 33 1st round picks were selected in the top 10, though no Buckeyes player has been drafted 1st overall since Orlando Pace in 1997. In 2006 and 2016, there were five Buckeyes among the 32 1st

round selections. Former Buckeyes were three of the top 10 picks in 2016, with Joey Bosa being drafted 3rd, Elliott being picked 4th, and Eli Apple rounding out the group as the 10th selection.

CHAPTER 12:

WRITING THE RECORD BOOK

QUIZ TIME!

1. How long is Archie Griffin's NCAA-record streak for consecutive games with at least 100 yards rushing?
   a. 30 games
   b. 31 games
   c. 32 games
   d. 33 games

2. Who did Eddie George gash for 314 yards in 1995 to become the first Buckeyes player to rush for 300 yards in a game?
   a. Penn State
   b. Purdue
   c. Illinois
   d. Minnesota

3. Who holds the record for most career rushing touchdowns at Ohio State?
   a. Pete Johnson
   b. Ezekiel Elliott

c. Keith Byars

d. Eddie George

4. What is the Ohio State record for most rushing touchdowns in a season?

   a. 20

   b. 22

   c. 23

   d. 25

5. Billy Anders and John Frank are the only two tight ends with at least 50 catches in a season in Ohio State history.

   a. True

   b. False

6. K.J. Hill and Gary Williams are tied in the Buckeyes record book for catching a pass in how many consecutive games?

   a. 48

   b. 46

   c. 44

   d. 42

7. David Boston holds the Ohio State single-season record for receiving yards.

   a. True

   b. False

8. What is Terry Glenn's record for most receiving yards in a game?

a. 234 yards

b. 246 yards

c. 253 yards

d. 267 yards

9. Who holds Ohio State's career passing yards record?

    a. Bobby Hoying

    b. Art Schlichter

    c. J.T. Barrett

    d. Joe Germaine

10. How many touchdown passes did Dwayne Haskins throw in 2018 to set the Big Ten single-season record?

    a. 41

    b. 44

    c. 47

    d. 50

11. Dwayne Haskins set the Ohio State record for completions and passing attempts in 2018 against Purdue when he finished with what stat line?

    a. 47 of 64

    b. 49 of 73

    c. 48 of 69

    d. 53 of 76

12. Who held the Ohio State record for most career passing touchdowns before J.T. Barrett destroyed it with 104 tosses?

    a. Art Schlichter

    b. Joe Germaine

c. Bobby Hoying

d. Troy Smith

13. No Ohio State player has ever had 15 sacks in a single season.

    a. True

    b. False

14. How many tackles did Tom Cousineau have against Penn State in 1978 and Chris Spielman have against Michigan in 1986 to share the school record for tackles in a game?

    a. 28

    b. 29

    c. 30

    d. 31

15. How many interceptions did Mike Sensibaugh have in his career to hold the Buckeyes' record?

    a. 18

    b. 19

    c. 21

    d. 22

16. In winning the Ray Guy Award as the best punter in the nation, which Ohio State punter set the school record for punt yardage in a season?

    a. Cameron Johnston

    b. Tom Tupa

    c. Brent Bartholomew

    d. B.J. Sander

17. Which kicking record does Mike Nugent NOT hold at Ohio State?

    a. Career made field goals
    b. Season made field goals
    c. Career attempted field goals
    d. Career field goal percentage

18. Who made the longest field goal in Ohio State history with a 59-yard kick?

    a. Drew Basil
    b. Dan Stultz
    c. Mike Nugent
    d. Tom Skladany

19. Mike Nugent is Ohio State's career scoring leader, but he did not pass a kicker to claim the record.

    a. True
    b. False

20. Who is the only Buckeyes returner to return two kickoffs for touchdowns in the same season?

    a. Dean Sensanbaugher
    b. Lenny Willis
    c. Ted Ginn Jr.
    d. Jeff Graham

QUIZ ANSWERS

1. B – 31 games

2. C – Illinois

3. A – Pete Johnson

4. D – 25

5. B – False

6. A – 48

7. A – True

8. C – 253 yards

9. C – J.T. Barrett

10. D – 50

11. B – 49 of 73

12. C – Bobby Hoying

13. B – False

14. B – 29

15. D – 22

16. D – B.J. Sander

17. C – Career attempted field goals

18. D – Tom Skladany

19. A – True

20. B – Lenny Willis

DID YOU KNOW?

1. On a day when Justin Fields and the passing game were not working for the Buckeyes, Trey Sermon led Ohio State to a critical win over Northwestern in the 2020 Big Ten championship game. Sermon ran 29 times for a school-record 331 yards against the Wildcats. He was at his best in the second half of that game with 271 yards on 22 carries. In the third quarter, he had rushes of 65 and 33 yards before giving the Buckeyes the lead for the first time with a nine-yard touchdown run. He had three more runs of more than 20 yards in the fourth quarter, and iced the game with a three-yard touchdown run midway through the period to secure Ohio State's spot in the College Football Playoff.

2. Archie Griffin's NCAA-record streak of 31 straight games with at least 100 yards rushing began and ended against the same opponent—Minnesota. In the 1973 season opener, Griffin romped for 129 yards on just 15 carries, and his final 100-yard performance came in the penultimate game of the 1975 regular season when he rushed for 124 yards against the Golden Gophers. It was Ohio State's rival to the north that ultimately stopped the streak by limiting Griffin to 46 yards on 19 carries, but, between those two Minnesota games, Griffin rushed for 4,359 yards, an average of more than 140 yards per game.

3. Terry Glenn made his first start of the 1995 season count against Pittsburgh en route to winning the Biletnikoff Award that season as the nation's best receiver. The speedster set the school record with 253 receiving yards and tied the record with four touchdowns as Ohio State trounced the Panthers that day. Glenn was the majority of the Buckeyes' passing attack as Bobby Hoying connected nine times for 253 yards with Glenn and six times for 41 yards to the other Ohio State receivers. Ironically, Glenn could not handle two punts early in the contest and muffed both of them before the Buckeyes recovered the live balls. But Glenn burned the Pittsburgh secondary, taking advantage of a speed mismatch that coach John Cooper said he was trying to exploit that day. It clearly worked, as Glenn caught touchdowns of 75, 61, and 36 yards in addition to an early 12-yard score.

4. It's surprising that David Boston was not a 1998 Biletnikoff finalist because he had a better season that year than Glenn did in 1995 when he won the award. Boston set the school record with 85 catches in 1998, and he still holds the record for single-season receiving yards with 1,435 yards, 24 more than Glenn had in 1995. Boston only hauled in 13 touchdowns that season, four off the pace Glenn set in 1995, but Boston had nine 100-yard games in 12 contests while Glenn had just seven in 13 games. Boston ranked third nationally in receiving yards and receiving touchdowns and seventh that season in catches.

5. There's something about playing Northwestern in the Big Ten title game that brings out the best in the Buckeyes. In the first meeting between the two schools in Indianapolis in 2018, Dwayne Haskins lit up the Wildcats secondary for a record 499 yards, easily surpassing the record he set earlier that season against Purdue. It was Haskins's fifth 400-yard performance of the season as he found the holes in the Northwestern zone and punished the Wildcats' aggressiveness. Haskins was under constant pressure and was sacked four times, but he also wiggled his way out of trouble several times to set up critical scores in the second half. He completed 34 of the 41 passes he was able to get off, and he threw for five touchdowns to survive a strong second-half push from the Wildcats to get the Buckeyes back to the Rose Bowl.

6. There was a giant secret around the Ohio State program heading into the 1978 season opener against Penn State because no one knew who would start at quarterback. Woody Hayes decided upon freshman hotshot Art Schlichter, and the decision did not look smart after the game. In his first collegiate game, Schlichter set the Ohio State record by throwing five interceptions against the Nittany Lions, one more than the number of touchdown passes he threw in the entire season. Schlichter went on to set the program record by tossing 21 interceptions that season, but he did gain 182 yards on just 12 completions against Penn State that day despite the shutout defeat.

7. Garcia Lane made history in 1983 when he returned two punts for touchdowns in a 33-22 win over Purdue. The scores were the second and third of Lane's Ohio State career and opened up the game for the Buckeyes in the third quarter. After the Buckeyes held the Boilermakers to a three-and-out on the opening possession of the second half, Lane fielded the punt at his own 37 and began to his left, made a quick cut back to his right, and then found the opening for a 63-yard punt return. On Purdue's third drive of the quarter, the Boilermakers again punted to Lane, and there was no need for cutbacks this time as he followed his blockers 71 yards for a touchdown. Only 10 Buckeyes have ever returned two punts for touchdowns in their career and only six of them did it in the same season.

8. When it comes to the Ohio State record book's section on kicking, Mike Nugent is basically atop every single list. His 120 points in 2002 has been surpassed four times since his graduation, but Nugent still holds the record for career points by a kicker (356), made field goals (72), career field goal percentage (81.8), and 50-yard field goals in a season (5) and career (8). Nugent also holds the top two spots with 25 field goals in 2002 and 24 in 2004. He made 24 straight field goals between 2001 and 2002, and he made two of the three 55-yard field goals by Ohio State kickers at home. He was the second Ohio State kicker to make five field goals in a game, tying the record with a perfect performance at North Carolina State in 2004, and

Nugent made eight of his nine kicks from at least 50 yards out.

9. In the finale of his Heisman Trophy-winning season, Vic Janowicz set a few records. Despite a swirling blizzard, Janowicz made the 27-yard field goal even though he could barely see the goalposts. He set records with his foot in a different way that day. He punted 21 times for 685 yards, marks that no one has come close to eclipsing in the more than 70 years since the infamous "Snow Bowl." Janowicz did have four punts blocked, both of which led to Michigan's only points in the game, but it was hard to blame him, given the conditions. After the game, Janowicz complained that his hands were frozen that made the game more difficult. "It was like a nightmare. My hands were numb (and blue). I had no feeling in them and I don't know how I hung onto the ball. It was terrible. You knew what you wanted to do, but you couldn't do it."

10. Before Tom Skladany trotting onto the field at the end of the first half against Illinois in 1975, Ohio State had had only one made field goal of 52 or more yards in its history. But with just a few seconds left and the Buckeyes only leading 7-3, Woody Hayes sent out Skladany for a 59-yard attempt. The kick sailed through the uprights, setting a new Big Ten record in the process. It still stands as the longest field goal in Ohio State history. In a 2012 interview, Skladany said that he knows modern kickers could easily surpass his record with their leg strength, but

the change in rules to spot the missed field goal at the previous line of scrimmage depresses the number of long field goals attempted in games.

CONCLUSION

Congratulations on reaching the end of this journey through the history of Ohio State football. Hopefully, the questions in the preceding 12 chapters tested your knowledge of Buckeyes football and expanded your horizons about your favorite team. If we've done our jobs well, you've reached this point filled to the brim with new facts about Ohio State, whether it's new information about the history of this storied program or learning stories from behind the scenes of your favorite moments in Ohio State football history. We certainly hope you enjoyed this trip through the history of the Buckeyes.

From its first games in the shadows of what is now Ohio Stadium through yet another appearance in the national championship game at the end of the 2020 season, the Ohio State University has provided the scarlet and gray faithful with plenty of exciting moments on the gridiron. Already this century, the Buckeyes have played for the national championship five times, winning a pair of them, and have been in the top 10 on many other occasions. Along the way, some exceptional players have worn the scarlet and gray for the Buckeyes, and there have been a few names that you likely want to forget. In the end, some of the best coaches in the history of college football coached the Buckeyes at some point, and, no matter who has been in charge, Ohio State football has remained the standard in the Big Ten.

We designed this book for you, the fans, to be able to embrace your favorite team and feel closer to them. Maybe you weren't familiar with what happened with Ohio State football before you became a fan. Perhaps you've lost touch with your alma mater in recent years, or you just wanted to re-live the glory days. This book was simply meant for your enjoyment, so no matter if you aced the quizzes or were stumped by them all, we hope you had fun and leave with more pride for the Buckeyes.

The 2020 season put a harsh spotlight on the Buckeyes due to the pandemic, but, through it all, the Buckeyes continued to prove their strength in reaching the national championship game again. Those who doubted the Buckeyes or criticized Ohio State's schedule were silenced by the performance of the players on the field. Ohio State again reigned supreme in the Big Ten and finally defeated Clemson after four tries before succumbing to Alabama. But, as is always the case in Columbus, the Buckeyes will be back in that spot soon enough, and someone else in the Big Ten is going to need to knock Ohio State off its throne atop the conference. Until that time, though, Ohio State is here to stay as a king of college football.

Made in the USA
Monee, IL
12 December 2021

84937028R00085